CHURCHILL'S
POLITICAL PHILOSOPHY

Churchill's Political Philosophy

BY

MARTIN GILBERT

THANK-OFFERING TO
BRITAIN FUND LECTURES
24, 25, *and* 27 *November*
1980

PUBLISHED FOR THE BRITISH ACADEMY
BY OXFORD UNIVERSITY PRESS
1981

Oxford University Press, Walton Street, Oxford OX2 6DP

London   Glasgow   New York   Toronto
Delhi   Bombay   Calcutta   Madras   Karachi
Kuala Lumpur   Singapore   Hong Kong   Tokyo
Nairobi   Dar es Salaam   Cape Town
Melbourne   Auckland

and associate companies in
Beirut   Berlin   Ibadan   Mexico City

Published in the United States by Oxford University Press, New York

ISBN 0 19 726005 5

Printed in Great Britain
at the University Press, Oxford
by Eric Buckley
Printer to the University

The sources of the documentary material used in this lecture include Churchill's wartime papers for the years 1940 to 1945, and the records of his first period at the Colonial Office, from 1905 to 1908 (both available at the Public Record Office, London); Churchill's own published works; Hansard, for all Parliamentary debates; newspaper and magazine articles by Churchill (at the British Library); and the following main and document volumes of the Churchill biography, published in Britain by William Heinemann, and in the United States by Houghton Mifflin:

Randolph S. Churchill, *Winston S. Churchill*, volume 1, 1874-1900 (1966)

Randolph S. Churchill, *Winston S. Churchill*, volume 1, documents (1967)

Randolph S. Churchill, *Winston S. Churchill*, volume 2, 1901-1914 (1967)

Randolph S. Churchill, *Winston S. Churchill*, volume 2, documents (1969)

Martin Gilbert, *Winston S. Churchill*, volume 3, 1914-1916 (1971)

Martin Gilbert, *Winston S. Churchill*, volume 3, documents (1972)

Martin Gilbert, *Winston S. Churchill*, volume 4, 1916-1922 (1975)

Martin Gilbert, *Winston S. Churchill*, volume 4, documents (1977)

Martin Gilbert, *Winston S. Churchill*, volume 5, 1923-1939 (1976)

Martin Gilbert, *Winston S. Churchill*, volume 5, document volume, 'The Exchequer Years' (1980)

Martin Gilbert, *Winston S. Churchill*, volume 5, document volume, 'The Wilderness Years' (1981)

Martin Gilbert, *Winston S. Churchill*, volume 5, document volume, 'The Coming of War' (1982)

CONTENTS

I

THE FORMATIVE YEARS
1894-1904

'LADIES of the Empire, I stand for Liberty.'

With these words Winston Churchill embarked on his first public speech. The Empire was not the British Empire—then almost at its widest extent—but the Empire Theatre, Leicester Square. Nor were the ladies the worthy matrons of some Imperial League, but ladies of ill repute whose activities in the lobby of the Empire had led to demands that the theatre itself be closed.

These demands had brought Churchill from Sandhurst, where he was a cadet, to London to speak against those whom he characterized as 'prudes on the prowl'. He was not quite twenty. But his intervention was more than a soldier's prank, and led him to the first public statement of his political and social ideas, in a letter to the *Westminster Gazette*, in which he argued that 'the improvement in the standard of public decency is due rather to improved social conditions and to the spread of education than to the prowling of the prudes'. Churchill went on to assert that what he called 'the only method of reforming human nature and of obtaining a higher standard of morality' lay neither in State penalties nor in the intervention of moralist bodies, but as he explained it, 'by educating the mind of the individual and improving the social conditions under which he lives'.

As Churchill saw it even in those youthful days, the dominant issue was liberty of the subject as against coercion and extremism. Both groups in the Empire Theatre dispute were anxious, he wrote, 'to see England better and more moral, but whereas the Vigilante Societies wish to abolish sin by Act of Parliament, and are willing to sacrifice much of the liberty of the subject into the bargain, the "anti-prudes" prefer a less coercive and more moderate procedure'.[1]

I would like to dwell on the youthful formation of Churchill's ideas, not only to show their evolution, but their remarkable clarity, vigour, and consistency. One aspect of Churchill's character from those earliest days was his constant questioning of the accepted view. The son of a Conservative household and family, he nevertheless warned his mother, after the Conservative election victory in 1895: 'to my mind they are too strong— Too brilliant altogether', and he added, with one of those insights which were to become so marked a feature of his thought: 'They are just the sort of Government to split on the question of Protection. Like a huge ship with powerful engines they will require careful steering— because any collision means destruction.'[2]

*   *   *

The base of Churchill's evolving philosophy was never theoretical. Between his twentieth and twenty-fifth birthday he travelled widely and had a series of varied and at times violent experiences in the United States, Cuba, India, the Sudan, and South Africa. On his first visit to the United States, in 1895, Churchill was struck by the strength of American society. Even the railway, cable car, and ferry systems, he wrote to one of his aunts, were 'harmoniously fitted into a perfect system accessible alike to the richest and the poorest'. It was this aspect of American capitalism which attracted him. 'When we reflect', he wrote, 'that such benefits have been secured to the people not by confiscation of the property of the rich or by arbitrary taxation but simply by business enterprise—out of which the promoters themselves have made colossal fortunes, one cannot fail to be impressed with the excellence of the active system.'[3] The United States, he told his brother, was 'not pretty or romantic, but great and utilitarian'. These were both virtues, but one area of American life he found distasteful, the extent of the discipline at West Point. After a visit there, learning of the restrictions on

[1] *The Westminster Gazette*, 18 October 1894.
[2] Letter of 3 August 1895, *Churchill*, document volume 1, page 582.
[3] Letter of 12 November 1895, *Churchill*, document volume 1, page 598.

pocket money, and the almost total absence of leave (only two months after the first two years), he wrote: 'In fact they have far less liberty than any private school boys in our country. I think such a state of things is positively disgraceful and young men of 24 or 25 who would resign their personal liberty to such an extent can never make good citizens or fine soldiers. A child who rebels against that sort of control should be whipped—so should a man who does not rebel.'[1]

When he wrote this Churchill was in fact on his way as a war correspondent to a war between a Colonial Government and rebels: the Spaniards and the Cubans. At first he had been critical of the actions of the rebels, writing in the first of his letters, for the *Daily Graphic*, that he doubted whether either 'restriction of liberty' or 'persistent bad Government' could justify the 'indescribable woe' caused by the burning of crops and farms.[2] And yet, he told his readers a few days later: 'The more I see of Cuba the more I feel sure that the end demand for independence is national and unanimous. The insurgent forces contain the best blood in the island, and can by no possible perversion of the truth be classed as banditti.'[3] But Churchill had no illusions even then about the nature of warfare. 'Whatever may be the result', he wrote, 'the suffering and misery of the entire community is certain.'[4]

This was Churchill's first experience of war. In fact, he was under rebel fire on his twenty-first birthday. And with each successive experience—in India, in Africa, and in Europe—he was to remain emphatic that, however just he, or society, might regard a war, it could only lead to suffering and misery.

Were the Cuban rebels right to rebel against Spain? Churchill's final reflection, in his last *Daily Graphic* article, was of sympathy for their situation. As he wrote:

There is no doubt that the island has been overtaxed in a monstrous manner for a considerable period. So much money is drawn from the country every year that industries are paralysed and development is

[1] Letter of 15 November 1895, *Churchill*, document volume 1, pages 599-600.
[2] *Daily Graphic*, 13 December 1895.
[3] Ibid., 17 December 1895.
[4] Ibid., 13 December 1895.

impossible. Nor is this all. The entire Administration is corrupt. All offices under the Government are reserved for Spaniards, who come to Cuba with the avowed intention of making their fortunes. Bribery and peculation pervade the boards of works, the post-offices, the Customs, and the courts of justice on a scale almost Chinese. A national and justifiable revolt is the only possible result of such a system.

Yet Churchill's experience of the rebel behaviour did not give him confidence in their abilities to form a Government. 'The only tactics they pursue', he wrote, 'are those of incendiaries and brigands—burning canefields, shooting from behind hedges, firing into sleeping camps, destroying property, wrecking trains, and throwing dynamite. These are perfectly legitimate in war, no doubt, but they are not acts on which States are founded.'[1]

*   *   *

In his address at the Empire Theatre Churchill had argued in favour of 'moderate procedure'. In a letter to his mother shortly before his twenty-second birthday he was to argue for a similar moderation in the evolution of British politics. As Churchill envisaged it, the party of the future would bring together the moderate wings of both Conservatism and Liberalism. But to this end the most moderate of the leaders of each side, Lord Rosebery and Joseph Chamberlain, would have to come together. As Churchill told his mother: 'Divided they would be curbed by the solid remnant of the Conservative party—peers, property publicans, parsons & turnips. Convergent interests would produce solidarity of action and their similar opinions would interpose no obstacle. Rosebery is only an advanced Tory—Chamberlain a prudent Radical. They would combine— and the fossils & the Fenians—the extremes of either party would be left in the cold'.[2]

In nearly sixty years of political life Churchill was never to have a Party affiliation in the accepted sense. Although he was to become a luminary in two great political Parties, and indeed the leader of one, he was never to feel entirely comfortable with the purely Party aspect of their activities, nor with the Party estab-

[1] *Daily Graphic*, 14 December 1895.
[2] Letter of 4 November 1896, *Churchill*, document volume 1, page 696.

lishment in either Party. His dream of a centre party of moderates, of a liberal and radical Toryism, never came to pass. In Party terms, he was always a little outside the accepted view: always seeking, but never finding, the middle way of his aspirations.

There was another aspect of his early philosophy that made him an uncomfortable partner in any political Party. In foreign affairs he adhered to the view that morality must, in the last resort, be the true guide, and that moral forces did exist. 'Do not let us mock at them,' he was to tell the House of Commons two years before the outbreak of the Second World War, in urging greater efforts for rearmament, 'for they are surely on our side. Do not mock at them, for this may well be a time when the highest idealism is not divorced from strategic prudence. Do not mock at them, for these may be the years, strange as it might seem, when Right may walk hand in hand with Might?'[1]

From what well of experience did Churchill reach these reflections?

It was events in the Mediterranean forty years before which first stirred Churchill's comments on international affairs and morality. When, in February 1897, the British Government supported the Turks, who were then suppressing a Greek uprising on the island of Crete, Churchill's reaction was support for the struggle of the victims. 'What an atrocious crime the Government have committed in Crete,' he wrote to his mother from India. 'That British warships should lead the way in protecting the blood bespattered Turkish soldiery from the struggles of their victims is horrible to contemplate.' And he accused the Government of having committed 'a crime, equally cruel and more shameless' than the action of Warren Hastings in the Rohilla war; a crime committed on this occasion 'in the full sight of the world and of history'.

For the first time since he had begun to follow Foreign affairs, Churchill found himself in agreement with the Liberal opposition. 'I cannot help hoping', he told his mother, 'that the Nemesis which waits on evil actions, may reduce and humble the perpetrators of such a crime.'[2]

---

[1] House of Commons, 4 March 1937.
[2] Letter of February 1897, *Churchill*, document volume 1, page 734.

Churchill's mother disagreed with his views on Crete. But he persisted in his belief that Britain's policy was wrong, writing to her some weeks later:

We are doing a very wicked thing in firing on the Cretan insurgents & in blockading Greece so that she cannot succour them. It will take a lot of whitewash to justify the spectacle of the Seaforth Highlanders fighting by the side of the Bashi Bazouk. I admit the material arguments are rather on the other side. That is bound to be the case. I look on this question from the point of view of right & wrong: Lord Salisbury from that of profit and loss.

Lord Salisbury's aim, Churchill added, was to bolster up Turkey in order to prevent the Russians seizing Constantinople. 'The Turkish Empire he is determined to maintain', and he added:

He does not care a row of buttons for the sufferings of those who are oppressed by that Empire. This is not only wrong but foolish. It is wrong because it is unjustifiable to kill people who are not attacking you—because their continued existence is inconvenient: and because it is an abominable action, which prolongs the servitude under the Turks of the Christian races.

Although he was a soldier, writing from his barracks in Bangalore, Churchill reflected on the political aspect of the Cretan crisis, and saw the Government as answerable for its victims. 'There are no lengths to which I would not go in opposing them', he told his mother, 'were I in the House of Commons', and he added: 'I am a Liberal in all but name. My views excite the pious horror of the Mess. Were it not for Home Rule—to which I will never consent—I would enter Parliament as a Liberal.'

Churchill then set out for his mother his evolving political philosophy, in the form of a definite programme: the extension of the franchise to every male, universal education, the equal establishment of all religions, wide measures of self-government, an eight-hour working day, and 'a progressive Income Tax' with the rate of tax increasing with the size of the income. Such, he said, was 'Reform at Home'. He was also in favour of what he called 'Imperialism abroad', telling his mother: 'East of Suez democratic reins are impossible. India must be governed on old principles.' And towards Europe, 'non-intervention. Keep absolutely unembroiled. Isolated if you like.'[1]

Such were Churchill's views at the age of twenty-two. He tested them against the accounts of the Bills of the 1870s in the *Annual Register*. Of the Artisans Dwelling Act of 1875 he wrote: 'Neither pity nor charity can inspire the Acts of a Government. The interest of the community alone must direct them.' As for the proposal of 1876 to exempt low incomes from income tax, Churchill wrote: 'I am strongly in favour of exemptions from this tax. Incomes earned by present work should also be more advantageously dealt with than inherited incomes.' Small incomes, he added, 'should not be taxed at all'.[2]

Churchill's Indian reflections also led him to favour universal manhood suffrage by raising the standard of education so that all classes would benefit. 'It will obviously be incumbent on the State', he wrote, to provide if required 'a meal for children under education'. No one, he insisted, 'can object to elevating the condition and improving the minds and harnessing the facilities of enjoyment of any class of human beings.' But it must not be forgotten, he warned, that for the majority of human beings, 'condemned to simple manual labour', an extensive education would 'excite desires which cannot be gratified and it will voice the desires in the language of discontent'.[3]

While these ideas, a mixture of the traditional and radical, were forming in Churchill's mind, he returned to England, and made his first political speech: to the Primrose League at Bath. He urged his Conservative audience to support the Government's Workmen's Compensation Bill, designed, as he put it, 'to protect workmen in dangerous trades from poverty if they became injured in the service of their employers'. The six thousand deaths at work each year made 'a terrible total'. The new law moved the question of compensation 'from the shifting sands of charity and placed it on the firm bedrock of law'.

[1] Letter of 6 April 1897, *Churchill*, document volume 1, pages 750-1.
[2] Notes pasted into the *Annual Register* for 1875, *Churchill*, document volume 1, page 762.
[3] Notes pasted into the *Annual Register* for 1876, *Churchill*, document volume 1, page 764.

Churchill then spoke of the engineers' strike that was then taking place. 'Whoever was right', he said, 'masters or men—both were wrong. Whoever might win, both must lose.' And he went on to tell his audience:

One of the questions which politicians had to face was how to avoid disputes between capital and labour. Ultimately he hoped that the labourer would become (as it were) a shareholder in the business in which he worked, and would not be unwilling to stand the pressure of a bad year because he shared some of the profits of a good one.

At the end of his speech Churchill criticized those who said that the British Empire had reached the height of its glory and power, and would now decline as Babylon, Carthage, and Rome had done. 'Do not believe these croakers', he said. The 'vigour and vitality' of the British race was unimpaired, and Britain would continue to bring 'peace, civilization and good government to the uttermost ends of the earth'.[1] Returning to India, Churchill wrote to his brother Jack: 'It is a proud reflection that all this vast expanse of fertile, populous country is ruled and administered by Englishmen. It is all the prouder when we reflect how complete and minute is the ruling—and how few are the rulers.'[2]

Yet this pride was quickly to be tempered by grim experience, for within two weeks of writing this letter, Churchill was in the midst of a war on the North-west Frontier, and witnessed all its terrors. 'There is no doubt we are a very cruel people', he wrote to a soldier friend. 'At Malakand the Sikhs put a wounded man into the cinerator and burnt him alive.'[3] And to his mother he wrote, after taking part in a series of fierce skirmishes: 'It is a war without quarter. They kill and mutilate everyone they catch and we do not hesitate to finish their wounded off.' As for himself, however, 'I have not soiled my hands with any dirty work.'[4]

Churchill did not restrict his criticisms to private letters. It

[1] *Bath Daily Chronicle*, 27 July 1897.
[2] Letter of 31 August 1898, *Churchill*, document volume 1, page 763.
[3] Letter to Reginald Barnes, 14 September 1897, *Churchill*, document volume 1, page 788.
[4] Letter of 2 October 1897, *Churchill*, document volume 1, page 797.

was always his belief that the truth should be made known, and that criticism should be in the open. During his period on the North-west Frontier the *Daily Telegraph* published fifteen of his long war dispatches; in one of these he urged the British politicians 'to lay their case frankly and fairly before the country, and trust to the courage and good sense of an ancient people'.[1] Nearly forty years later he was to tell the House of Commons: 'No doubt it is not popular to say these things, but I am accustomed to abuse and I expect to have a great deal more of it before I have finished. Somebody has to state the truth.'[2]

From India, Churchill continued to state the truth as he saw it. The policy of annexing neutral territory, he told his mother, had made the Malakand uprising inevitable. Of the policy itself he wrote: 'Financially it is ruinous. Morally it is wicked. Militarily it is an open question, and politically it is a blunder.'[3] Although he had himself been in action, he understood the point of view of the tribesmen, resisting 'when their country was invaded and their property destroyed'. And when a spokesman for Lord Lansdowne denied the extent of deaths from disease among the British troops, Churchill told his mother: 'Lord Lansdowne knows this as well as we do—and he should not lend himself to a policy of misrepresentation.'[4]

The savagery of the war on the North-west Frontier made an indelible impression on Churchill. But how was he to get his views across to a wider public? The very fact that he had seen action on the North-west Frontier must, he believed, 'give me more weight politically, must add to my claims to be listened to'.[5] The fact that he had been under fire ten times, and in three sharp skirmishes, would, he believed, be 'Quite a foundation for a political life'.[6]

Churchill was also realizing his gift for oratory, and the uses to which it could be put. Of the power of oratory he wrote, at the

[1] *Daily Telegraph*, 6 November 1897.
[2] Speech to the City Carlton Club, 26 September 1935, quoted in Gilbert, *Churchill*, volume 5, page 669.
[3] Letter to his mother, 21 October 1897, *Churchill*, document volume 1, page 807.
[4] Letter to his mother, 19 January 1898, *Churchill*, document volume 1, page 860.
[5] Letter to his mother, 29 August 1897, *Churchill*, document volume 1, page 780.
[6] Letter to his mother, 12 October 1897, *Churchill*, document volume 1, page 804.

time of his twenty-third birthday: 'He who enjoys it wields a power more durable than that of a great king. He is an independent force in the world. Abandoned by his party, betrayed by his friends, stripped of his offices, whoever can command this power is still formidable.' It was untrue, he asserted, that the power of personality in politics was a thing of the past. 'Human weakness appears to be one of the few unvarying features of life.' The orator would always be powerful, embodying as he did 'the passions of the multitude'. But before he could inspire others with any emotion, 'he must be swayed by it himself. When he could rouse their indignation, his heart is filled with anger. Before he can move their tears, his own must flow. To convince them, he must himself believe.'

A skilful orator, Churchill added, could either 'translate an established truth into simple language', or 'adventurously aspire to reveal the unknown'.[1]

Churchill's concept of oratory was to become an integral part of his political philosophy: oratory to inspire the multitude, and at the same time, valueless unless it reflected the passions of the multitude. All his life, it was the passions, the issues, rather than the personalities, or the political calculations, which determined Churchill's involvement. 'It is a great comfort', he was to write to his son in 1931, 'when one minds the questions one cares about far more than office or Party or friendships.'[2] 'As long as I am fighting a cause', he told a friend, also in 1931, 'I am not afraid of anything. Nor do I weary as the struggle proceeds.'[3] As to his apparently total political isolation of the time of the Abdication, 'I do not feel', he wrote to Bernard Baruch, 'that my own political position is much affected by the line I took; but even if it were, I should not have acted otherwise. As you know, in politics I always prefer to accept the guidance of my heart to calculations of public feeling.'[4]

Clearly, in 1940, this 'guidance of the heart' was to coincide

---

[1] Unpublished article, 'The Scaffolding of Rhetoric', *Churchill*, document volume 1, pages 816–21.

[2] Letter of 8 January 1931, *Churchill*, document volume 'The Wilderness Years'.

[3] Letter of 3 February 1931, to Lord Rothermere, *Churchill*, document volume 'The Wilderness Years'.

[4] Letter of 1 January 1937, *Churchill*, document volume 'The Coming of War'.

with the national will. And as early as 1906, in his biography of his father, Churchill had expressed his confidence in a real England which did not depend upon Party, or 'calculations':

Lord Randolph Churchill's name will not be recorded upon the bead-roll of either party. The Conservatives, whose forces he so greatly strengthened, the Liberals, some of whose finest principles he notably sustained, must equally regard his life and work with mingled feelings. A politician's character and position are measured in his day by party standards. When he is dead, all that he achieved in the name of party, is at an end. The eulogies and censures of partisans are powerless to affect his ultimate reputation. The scales wherein he was weighed are broken. The years to come bring weights and measures of their own.

There is an England which stretches far beyond the well-drilled masses who are assembled by party machinery to salute with appropriate acclamation the utterances of their recognised fuglemen; an England of wise men who gaze without self-deception at the failings and follies of both political parties; of brave and earnest men who find in neither faction fair scope for the effort that is in them; of 'poor men' who increasingly doubt the sincerity of party philanthropy. It was to that England that Lord Randolph Churchill appealed; it was that England he so nearly won; it is by that England he will be justly judged.[1]

As Churchill's personal and political philosophy was being formed on the North-west Frontier, and in the barracks at Bangalore, his mind had turned increasingly to politics. But he was aware that to enter politics it was not enough to have had adventures, experience, and influence. As he wrote to his mother early in 1898:

In Politics a man, I take it, gets on not so much by what he *does*, as by what he *is*. It is not so much a question of brains as of character & originality. It is for these reasons that I would not allow others to suggest ideas and that I am somewhat impatient of advice as to my beginning in politics. Introduction—connections—powerful friends— a name—good advice well followed—all these things count—but they lead only to a certain point. As it were they may ensure admission to the scales. Ultimately—every man has to be weighed—and if found wanting nothing can procure him the public confidence.

[1] Winston S. Churchill, *Lord Randolph Churchill*, London 1906, volume 2, pages 488-9.

Nor would I desire it under such circumstances. If I am not good enough—others are welcome to take my place. I should never care to bolster up a sham reputation and hold my position by disguising my personality. Of course—as you have known for some time—I believe in myself. If I did not I might perhaps take other views.[1]

*   *   *

It was the war in the Sudan that was to prove decisive in Churchill's philosophy. At first Churchill's instinct was eagerness to see action. 'I have a keen aboriginal desire', he told his mother, 'to kill several of these odious dervishes.' And he added: 'I anticipate enjoying the exercise very much.'[2] Nearing the battle zone, he wrote again: 'I am very happy and contented and eagerly looking forward to the approaching actions.'[3] And after the battle of Omdurman he commented, on the cavalry charge itself, 'I told my troop they were the finest men in the world and I am sure they would have followed me as far as I would have gone and that I may tell you and you only—was a very long way—for my soul becomes very high in such moments.'[4]

Yet even as he wrote this letter, Churchill was beginning work on his book, *The River War*, in which he was to stress the cruelties of war; and it was these cruelties which made so deep an imprint on his mind. Describing to his mother the actual events of the battlefield and the way in which several of his friends had been killed and mutilated, he wrote of how these things had made him 'anxious and worried during the night and I speculated on the shoddiness of war. You cannot gild it. The raw comes through.'[5]

Such sentiments did not remain in the shelter of a private letter. In *The River War* itself Churchill told his readers:

The statement that 'the wounded Dervishes received every delicacy and attention' is so utterly devoid of truth that it transcends the limits

[1] Letter of 26 January 1898, from Bangalore, *Churchill*, document volume 1, pages 863-4.
[2] Letter of 10 August 1898, written on the Nile, *Churchill*, document volume 1, page 963.
[3] Letter of 19 August 1898, on the Nile, *Churchill*, document volume 1, page 968.
[4] Letter of 17 September 1898, *Churchill*, document volume 1, page 981.
[5] Letter of 4 September 1898, *Churchill*, document volume 1, page 974.

of mendacity and passes into the realms of the ridiculous. I was impatient to get back to the camp. There was nothing to be gained by dallying on the field, unless a man were anxious to become quite callous, so that no imaginable misery which could come to human flesh would ever have moved him again. I may have written in these pages something of vengeance and of the paying of a debt. It may be that vengeance is sweet, and that the gods forbade vengeance to men because they reserved for themselves so delicious and intoxicating a drink. But no one should drain the cup to the bottom. The dregs are often filthy-tasting.[1]

Churchill was never to abandon these feelings, which continued also to be a feature of his private letters. 'The treatment of the wounded', he wrote to his mother 'again disgraceful.'[2] And of Kitchener: 'A vulgar common man—without much of the non-brutal elements in his composition.'[3] The writing of *The River War* forced Churchill to the decision which confronts all authors: should one perpetuate in print what one says in the transient privacy of letters or conversation. After careful reflection, Churchill decided to print the truth as he saw it, that the victory at Omdurman, as he told his mother, 'was disgraced by the inhuman slaughter of the wounded and that Kitchener is responsible for this'.[4] And in *The River War* itself Churchill wrote: 'The stern and unpitying spirit of the commander was communicated to his troops, and the victories which marked the progress of the River War were accompanied by acts of barbarity not always justified even by the harsh customs of savage conflicts or the fierce and treacherous nature of the Dervish.'[5]

The realization that opinions such as these would be unpopular did not deter Churchill from publishing them. 'I do not think the book will bring me many friends', he wrote to his cousin Ivor Guest. 'But friends of the cheap and worthless every-day variety are not of very great importance. After all in writing the great thing is to be honest.'[6]

[1] *The River War*, London 1899.
[2] Letter of 16 September 1898, *Churchill*, document volume 1, page 979.
[3] Letter of 29 December 1898, *Churchill*, document volume 1, page 997.
[4] Letter of 26 January 1899, *Churchill*, document volume 1, page 1004.
[5] *The River War*, London 1899.
[6] Letter of 19 January 1899, Satinoff papers, *Churchill*, document volume 2, pages xxv–vi.

While writing *The River War*, Churchill spoke to many of the participants in the political struggles of Egypt and the Sudan, including one of the leading Egyptian nationalists. Indeed, he had begun, at the age of twenty-four, to understand, as many of his contemporaries failed to understand, that the enemy of today, hated in the heat of battle, was not necessarily the enemy of tomorrow; and that the moment of triumph of the victors was also the moment of their greatest test.

In Cairo, while writing his book, Churchill wrote to his mother:

I am going to lunch to-day with Tigrane Pasha who represents the patriotic party here and who would be very glad to see the last of the British in Egypt. He is, I believe, a very honest man and is quite prepared to talk frankly and to air his views. Lord Cromer is on friendly terms with him. He says it is great nonsense to talk about these people as being 'disloyal'. Why we should however expect them to be 'loyal' is quite beyond his comprehension.[1]

Churchill had also refused to share the anti-Semitism of many of his relatives and closest friends. 'Bravo Zola!' he had written in 1898, when the accusations against Dreyfus were successfully challenged. 'I am delighted to witness the complete debacle of that monstrous conspiracy.'[2] And as the scandal dragged on, and the full extent of anti-Jewish feeling in France became clear, he had expostulated: '. . . such a drama—with real flesh and blood for properties. What a vile nation the French are. Nature must vindicate herself by letting them die out.'[3]

In 1905 he was to be a leading public speaker against Tsarist persecution of the Jews. In 1908 he was to describe Jerusalem as 'the only ultimate goal' for the Jewish people.[4] In 1920 he had urged Yudenitch in the Baltic, and Denikin in the Ukraine, to halt their killing of Jews, and to issue 'a proclamation against anti-Semitism'.[5] In 1942 he warned one of his closest personal

[1] Letter of 3 April 1899, *Churchill*, document volume 1, page 1020.
[2] Letter of 8 September 1898, written at Omdurman, *Churchill*, document volume 1, page 976.
[3] Letter of 13 August 1899, *Churchill*, document volume 2, page 104.
[4] Letter of 30 January 1908, quoted in Gilbert, *Churchill*, volume 4, page 484.
[5] See Gilbert, *Churchill*, volume 4, pages 293, 330, 341–3, and 351.

friends 'against drifting into the usual anti-Zionist and anti-Semitic channel which it is customary for British officials to follow'.[1] It was the German deportation of the Jews that he described—in the summer of 1942—as 'the most bestial, the most squalid, the most senseless of all their offences'—the one which, in his view, 'illustrates as nothing else can the utter degradations of the Nazi nature and theme . . .'.[2]

*   *   *

At the age of twenty-five and a half, Churchill stood for Parliament, but was defeated. In his Election Address he described himself as a Tory Democrat, and stated that the 'main end of modern government' was 'the improvement of the condition of the British people'. In his Address he also pledged himself to promote, to the best of his ability, 'all legislation which, without throwing the country into confusion and disturbing the present concord, and without impairing that tremendous energy of production on which the wealth of the nation and the good of the people depend, may yet raise the standard of happiness and comfort in English homes'.[3]

Four months after his defeat at the polls Churchill was on his way to South Africa as a war correspondent. And it was in South Africa that the pre-political evolution of his ideas was completed.

Churchill's attitude to the Boers was again quite unlike that of the mass of Conservatives, or of his fellow officers. 'It is astonishing how we have underrated these people', he wrote to the Adjutant-General, Sir Evelyn Wood,[4] and within a week Churchill himself had been captured. 'I confess myself much impressed', he wrote from prison in Pretoria to the Prince of Wales, 'with their courtesy, courage and humanity. At the end they could easily have shot us all down, and we by continuing our fight showed that we had no intention of surrendering. Instead of destroying us, they galloped in amongst the fugitives—

---

[1] Premier Papers, 4/52/5, Prime Minister's Personal Minute DM 1/2 of 11 September 1942.

[2] House of Commons, 8 September 1942.

[3] Election Address, 24 June 1899, *Churchill*, document volume 1, page 1030.

[4] Letter of 10 November 1899, Natal Government Archives, printed in *Churchill*, document volume 1, page 1058.

at considerable risk to themselves—and so persuaded as much as compelled us to become prisoners.'[1]

Later, having escaped from prison, and rejoined the British forces, Churchill wrote immediately after the relief of Ladysmith: 'I would treat the Boers with all generosity and tolerance, even to providing for those crippled in the war and for the destitute women and children.'[2]

Once more, Churchill's personal experience of warfare made a fierce impact. 'The scenes on Spion Kop', he wrote in a private letter, 'were among the strangest and most terrible I have ever witnessed',[3] and in one of his dispatches for the *Morning Post* he wrote, after describing the sight of the dead Boers at Trichardt's Drift, following a British victory: 'Ah, horrible war, amazing medley of the glorious and the squalid, the pitiful and the sublime, if modern men of light and leading saw your face closer, simple folk would see it hardly ever.'[4]

Even while the war was still being fought, Churchill published a letter in the *Natal Witness* appealing for moderation in the post-war settlement:

A cry, growing into a clamouring, which I can perfectly understand, has arisen that stern retribution should be meted out to these guilty and miserable people. I read your newspapers and the reports of recent meetings industriously and all reveal the same spirit. 'Give them a lesson they will never forget'. 'Make an example.' 'Condign punishment'. 'Our turn now.' These are the phrases or ideas which recur. It is the spirit of revenge. It is wrong, first of all because it is morally wicked; and secondly because it is practically foolish. Revenge may be sweet, but it is also most expensive.

While we continue to prosecute the war with tireless energy and remorselessly beat down all who resist—to the last man if necessary— we must also make it easy for the enemy to accept defeat. We must tempt as well as compel. On the one hand the Dutchman may see vast

---

[1] Letter of 30 November 1899, Royal Archives, printed in *Churchill*, document volume 1, page 1081.

[2] Letter of 22 March 1900, recipient unknown, *Churchill*, document volume 1, page 1160.

[3] Letter of 28 January 1900, to Miss Pamela Plowden, Lytton papers, printed in *Churchill*, document volume 1, page 1147.

[4] Published in Winston S. Churchill, *London to Ladysmith via Pretoria*, London 1900, page 292.

armies equipped with all the terrible machinery of war advancing irresistibly; on the other the quiet tin-roofed farm half buried in the trees far from the roar of conflict and the dread of death. . . .

Beware of driving men to desperation. Even a cornered rat is dangerous. We desire a speedy peace and the last thing in the world we want is that this war should enter upon a guerilla phase. Those who demand 'an eye for an eye and a tooth for a tooth' should ask themselves whether such barren spoils are worth five years of bloody partisan warfare and the consequent impoverishment of South Africa.

'Do not act or speak', Churchill added, 'so that it may be said "It is true, the Natal colonists have fought well; but they were drunk with racial animosity. They were brave in battle; but they are spiteful in victory." '[1]

These sentiments were expressed both forcefully, and publicly, bringing down on Churchill the anger of the newspaper, and of many South African whites. But Churchill defended his stance, and to one of those who had been angered by his advocacy of a lenient policy he wrote:

Perhaps this is not the time to write of mercy and forgiveness. But you know perfectly well the spirit that I protested against. It disgusts me. Looking on South African matters with an eye which if it be not trained by long experience is nevertheless undimmed by prejudice, I find much to admire in the Dutch. I regard them as an essential to the development and prosperity of South Africa: and I do not want to associate myself with any—natural if you like—ebullition of racial animosity on the part of their British fellow colonists. . . .[2]

Churchill's religious views were likewise influenced by what he regarded as the conflict between moderation and extremism. To his former headmaster, the Reverend (later Bishop) Weldon, he had written at the end of 1896, in a letter arguing against Christian missionary work in India:

Had I lived in the days when the influence of Buddha—of Christ—or of Mahomet began to disturb these primitive forms of worship—I should probably have opposed—though I could not have impeded—

[1] Natal Witness, 29 March 1900, published in *Churchill*, document volume 1, pages 1162-4.
[2] Letter of 13 April 1900, to Rae Collins, *Churchill*, document volume 1, pages 1169-70.

the great movements they initiated. And this would have been my reason—that though these religions were in every case more worthy of God and man—than those they superseded—yet the change would be attended with deluges of blood and floods of theological controversy— extending over hundreds of years—during which period the sum of human happiness and prosperity would be appreciably diminished. The event would have justified these anticipations. *We* regard the turmoil from a different standpoint. Other generations have paid the price—we enjoy the benefit: The crown which the martyr himself deserved has been awarded to his posterity: and looking backward from our own time we can feel nothing but gratitude to those who have conferred upon our contemporaries—incalculable blessings—which have cost us nothing. But I should not have been prepared to have paid the price then—nor do I approve of it being exacted—on a smaller scale—now.[1]

Churchill's view of turn-of-the-century Catholicism was likewise censorious. Oxford, he told his brother Jack—who aspired to a University education, 'has long been the home of bigotry and intolerance and has defended more damnable errors and wicked notions than any other institution, with the exception of the Catholic Church . . .'.[2]

A year later, however, in a letter to his cousin Ivor Guest, Churchill advised his cousin not to intervene, as a Protestant partisan, in the ritualist controversy then raging.

. . . as a rationalist I deprecate all Romish practices and prefer those of Protestantism, because I believe that the Reformed Church is less deeply sunk in the mire of dogma than the Original Establishment. We are at any rate a step nearer Reason.

But at the same time I can see a poor parish—working men living their lives in ugly white-washed factories, toiling day after day amid scenes & surroundings destitute of the element of beauty. I can sympathise with their aching longing for something not infected by the general squalor & something to gratify their love of the mystic, something a little nearer to the 'all-beautiful'—and I find it hard to rob their lives of this one ennobling aspiration—even though it finds

[1] Letter of 16 December 1896, from Bangalore, *Churchill*, document volume 1, pages 712–14.
[2] Letter of 13 January 1898, on the train between Bangalore and Calcutta, *Churchill*, document volume 1, page 858.

expression in the burning of incense, the wearing of certain robes and other superstitious practices.

Such were Churchill's reasons for not entering the controversy. But his anti-Catholic opinions had gained in strength and argument. As he wrote to his cousin:

... I know that these indulgences are enervating: that peoples that think much of the next world rarely prosper in this: that men must use their minds and not kill their doubts by sensuous pleasures: that superstitious faith in nations rarely promotes their industry: that, in a phrase, Catholicism—all religions if you like, but particularly Catholicism—is a delicious narcotic. It may soothe our pains and chase our worries, but it checks our growth and saps our strength.

'And since the improvement of the British breed is my political aim in life', Churchill added, 'I would not permit too great indulgence if I could prevent it without assailing another great principle—Liberty.'[1]

Catholicism versus Liberty was also the theme of his comment on Mrs Humphrey Ward's new novel, *Helbeck of Bannisdale*. 'I was so thankful', he wrote of the heroine, 'when the girl committed suicide. It would have been too cruel had she resigned her free spirit, covered her brain with cobwebs and become a Catholic.'[2]

*   *   *

Churchill's instinct not to echo the popular cry of the hour, or to mouth the prejudice of the day, was an important facet of his evolving philosophy. He was never one to cling to opinions for the sake of consistency. 'The word "Afterwards" fills one with all sorts of doubts and perplexity,' he wrote from his prison in Pretoria, 'and I find it the harder to make up my mind the more I learn and see.'[3] And even as the British victories in South Africa had mounted, he still remained, as we have seen, unwilling to follow the prevailing view. 'I have tried to form my

[1] Letter of 19 January 1899, Satinoff papers, *Churchill*, document volume 2, pages xxvi–vii.

[2] Letter of 5 August 1898, to his mother, *Churchill*, document volume 1, page 958.

[3] Letter to the Prince of Wales, 30 November 1899, Royal Archives, *Churchill*, document volume 1, pages 1080–2.

own opinions on the state of affairs and society here', he wrote to Joseph Chamberlain in April 1900, 'without accepting the usual formulas, and in consequence I have many doubts.'[1] Eight years later he was to write to his fiancée:

> I never put too much trust in formulas & classifications. The human mind & still more human speech are vy inadequate to do justice to the infinite variety & complexity of phenomena. Women so rarely realise this. When they begin to think they are so frightfully cock-sure. Now nature never deals in black or white. It is always some shade of grey. She never draws a line without smudging it. And there must be a certain element of give & play even about the most profound & assured convictions.[2]

One subject on which Churchill had found time to reflect while he had been in prison in Pretoria was the relationship between capitalism and the individual, writing on his twenty-fifth birthday to a Republican friend in America:

> . . . capitalism in the form of Trusts has reached a pitch of power which the old economists never contemplated and which excites my most lively terror. Merchant-princes are all very well, but if I have anything to say to it, their kingdom shall not be of this world. The new century will witness the great war for the existence of the Individual. Up to a certain point combination has brought us nothing but good: but we seem to have reached a period when it threatens nothing but evil. I do not want to see men buy cheaper food & better clothes at the price of their manhood.

'Poor but independent', Churchill added, 'is worth something as a motto',[3] and a year later, while standing as a Conservative at Oldham, he expressed his sympathy for the Lancashire manufacturers who had joined together 'to try to break the necks of those odious American Corners which hold up cotton of a very inferior quality to a high price'.[4]

*   *   *

[1] Letter of 7 April 1900, Joseph Chamberlain papers, *Churchill*, document volume 1, pages 1167-8.

[2] Letter of 16 April 1908 to Clementine Hozier, Lady Spencer-Churchill papers, published in *Churchill*, document volume 2, page 782.

[3] Letter of 30 November 1899, to Bourke Cochran, *Churchill*, document volume 1, page 1083.

[4] Letter of 8 September 1900, to his mother, *Churchill*, document volume 1, page 1198.

On 14 February 1901 Churchill took his seat in Parliament. Now was the time when all his youthful opinions, and all his self-confidence, were to be put to the test. Now he was to have to match his evolving philosophy with the wants and controversies of the day, and to decide which issues, old and new, were to be the ones on which to make a stand. But on the immediate issue, peace with the Boers, his belief that the harshness of war should be followed by a magnanimous peace, was already well formed, and in his maiden speech, made only four days after he had entered the House of Commons, he declared: 'If there were persons who rejoiced in this war, and went out with hopes of excitement or the lust of conflict, they have had enough, and more than enough today.' It should now be made 'easy and honourable' for the Boers to surrender.[1]

Commenting on Churchill's attitude, *Punch* praised what it called his 'gift' of 'viewing familiar objects from a new stand-point', as well as his 'shrewd, confident judgement'.[2] But the appeal for magnanimity towards the Boers was challenged by many Conservatives in Britain just as it had been by those of English stock in South Africa. In a public letter defending his views Churchill declared: 'Neither side has a monopoly of right or reason.'[3]

Jingoism, however, still flourished, and with it an emotional demand that the war must go on until the last pocket of Boer resistance was crushed. Speaking in Yorkshire, Churchill set out his argument against allowing the war to drag on and on and on:

. . . now there is a most perilous apathy. We seem to regard the war as chronic. Public attention is often diverted from it. The visit of an Emperor to a neighbouring State, the murder of a President on the other side of the Atlantic; yes, even such things as the racing of pleasure yachts, turns the minds of thousands from the great public undertaking which we are pledged to carry through.

Gentlemen, I appeal to you never to let the war pass out of your minds for a day. Think what it means to us all. Friends, brothers, or sons, fighting and toiling, ragged and hungry, while the weeks pass by,

---

[1] House of Commons, 18 February 1901.
[2] *Punch*, 27 February 1901.
[3] *Westminster Gazette*, 18 March 1901.

while summer grows out of spring, and autumn withers into winter. How many are there here to-night who may look in the newspaper tomorrow morning to find, as I found last week, some familiar name, and learn that some bright eye known and trusted is closed for ever.

Then there is the money, the wealth of the nation, draining away, drip, drip, drip—enough to buy every month four of the largest battleships in the world. There is India. Nearly thirty thousand men detained beyond their contract with the State impatiently await relief in India.

Every day increases the strain on your military organisation, and the embarrassment of your finances. The loyal districts of South Africa sicken in the grip of martial law; the gulf of hatred between Boer and Briton grows wider; and every day devastation and ruin rule over larger areas.

'Surely', Churchill added, 'if ever a supreme effort were needed to terminate or curtail this time of trouble, it is needed now.'[1]

Conscious of the enormous energy which the nation had put into making war, Churchill was also evolving a view of the transfer of such energies to peace-making needs. In his first Parliamentary amendment he argued that, 'while fully recognising the necessity of providing adequately for Imperial defence', the House of Commons nevertheless 'cannot view without grave apprehension the continued growth of purely military expenditure which diverts the energies of the country from their natural commercial and military development'.[2] The material need, he explained a week later in a letter to *The Times*, was for 'measures of social development and reform'. Such reforms, he believed, would have the effect of 'stimulating and sustaining the spirit of the people'.[3]

Within three months of entering Parliament, Churchill had emerged as a leading opponent of increased military expenditure, now that the war in South Africa was drawing to a close. Reflecting on the virtual doubling on military spending in the previous twenty years, he asked the House of Commons: 'Has the wealth of the country doubled?' 'Is there no poverty at

---

[1] Speech at Saddleworth, Yorkshire, 4 October 1901, quoted in *Churchill*, document volume 2, pages 83–90.

[2] *The Times*, 23 April 1901.

[3] Ibid., 3 May 1901.

home?' 'Is the revenue so easily raised that we do not know how
to spend it?' 'Are the Treasury buildings pulled down and all
our financiers fled?' As for the constant war talk, the stock-in-
trade of the jingos, Churchill declared:

We must not regard war with a modern Power as a kind of game in
which we may take a hand, and with good luck and good management
may play adroitly for an evening and come safe home with our
winnings. It is not that, and I rejoice that it cannot be that. A
European war cannot be anything but a cruel, heartrending struggle,
which, if we are ever to enjoy the bitter fruits of victory, must demand,
perhaps for several years, the whole manhood of the nation, the entire
suspension of peaceful industries, and the concentrating to one end of
every vital energy in the community.

I have frequently been astonished since I have been in this House
to hear with what composure and how glibly Members, and even
Ministers, talk of a European war. I will not expatiate on the horrors of
war, but there has been a great change which the House should not
omit to notice. In former days, when wars arose from individual
causes, from the policy of a Minister or the passion of a King, when
they were fought by small regular armies of professional soldiers, and
when their course was retarded by the difficulties of communication
and supply, and often suspended by the winter season, it was possible
to limit the liabilities of the combatants. But now, when mighty
populations are impelled on each other, each individual severally
embittered and inflamed—when the resources of science and civilisation sweep away everything that might mitigate their fury, a European
war can only end in the ruin of the vanquished and the scarcely less
fatal commercial dislocation and exhaustion of the conquerors.
Democracy is more vindictive than Cabinets. The wars of peoples will
be more terrible than those of kings . . .

Foreign nations know what war is. There is scarcely a capital in
Europe which has not been taken in the last one hundred years, and
it is the lively realisation of the awful consequences of war which
maintains the peace of Europe. We do not know what war is. We have
had a glimpse of it in South Africa. Even in miniature it is hideous
and appalling; but, for all our experience, war to us does not mean
what it means to the Frenchman, or the German, or the Austrian. Are
we not arming ourselves with their weapons without being under their
restraints?

What I fear is that these three costly and beautiful army corps which are to be kept ready—almost at a moment's notice—for foreign war will develop in the country, if they need developing, feelings of pride and power, which will not only be founded in actual military superiority, but only on the appearance of it. And in these days, when popular newspapers, appealing with authority to countless readers, are prepared almost every morning to urge us into war against one or other—and sometimes several—of the Great Powers of the earth, surely we ought not to make it seem so easy, and even attractive, to embark on such terrible enterprises, or to think that with the land forces at our disposal we may safely intermeddle in the European game?

Britain's security, Churchill argued, was twofold. The first was the Royal Navy; the second, the 'moral force' of Britain; for, as Churchill said, 'in spite of every calumny and lie uttered or printed, the truth comes to the top, and it is known alike by peoples and by rulers that on the whole British influence is healthy and kindly, and makes for the general happiness and welfare of mankind'. It would be a 'fatal bargain', he added, for the sake of unnecessary military expenditure, to allow this moral force 'to become diminished, or perhaps even destroyed'.[1]

Churchill already had a clear picture of what lay behind this 'healthy and kindly British influence'. There was, he wrote in a newspaper article in the summer of 1901, a single story linking the 'many and varied' events of British history, and this was the story of 'free institutions, developing manhood and commerce; commerce impatient of island limits going down to the sea in ships and breeding fleets; sea-power preserving us from Continental tumult, stimulating manufacture anew . . .'. Not military or even naval power, but commercial strength, was Britain's heart. 'We have survived defeat before', he wrote. 'We have even risen stronger from the loss of our greatest possession. But the collapse of trade would be fatal.'[2]

*   *   *

During Churchill's first three years in Parliament he remained, as he had been elected, a Conservative. But it was during those three years, between his twenty-sixth and twenty-

---

[1] House of Commons, 13 May 1901.
[2] *Daily Mail*, 17 June 1901.

ninth birthdays, that his political ideas evolved into their mature frame. By his thirtieth birthday he had formally joined the Liberal Party, and only a few days after his thirty-first birthday he had been appointed a junior Minister in a Liberal Government.

This evolution, although rapid, arose naturally out of his earlier attitude and expressions, and was in harmony with the ideas which had now begun to form themselves in the testing arena of Parliament, where Churchill believed it necessary not only to expound, but to explain: an aspect of the democratic process to which he remained committed throughout his life.

The concept of truth withheld was always to distress him, whether it was the question of military conduct in the Boer War, or the extent of German rearmament more than thirty years later. 'Tell the Truth to the British People', Lord Birkenhead's phrase about India, was to become Churchill's own slogan about rearmament in the nineteen-thirties. An early version of it is found in a lecture which he delivered in the autumn of 1901:

I am not afraid of the British public getting panic stricken. The London clubs may hum with excitement, the political wire pullers may be perfectly frantic, the Stock Exchange may be in hysterics, but John Bull is a very stolid person. He has lived long enough to see the day break bright & fair after many a stormy night. He will not be frightened. I would say to the Govt—take him into your confidence. Let him know the whole truth; and you will derive a real encouragement in the tremendous task that lies before, wh restores the fortune of the British Empire, proves the consciousness of the comradeship and sympathy of millions of the most sensible people in the world.

There are enormous and incalculable resources of energy, strength, and self denial in this people—resources equal to overcoming far greater perils than now confront us, if only the Govt has the power to call them forth.[1]

Churchill was equally emphatic in setting out his concept of truth to the House of Commons, and in doing so angered those fellow Conservatives whose attitudes and behaviour he was criticizing without reserve:

[1] Churchill papers, Press Cutting Albums.

Perhaps it will not be entirely agreeable to many of my friends on this side of the House if I say that I have noticed in the last three wars in which we have been engaged a tendency among military officers—arising partly from good nature towards their comrades, partly from the dislike of public scrutiny—to hush everything up, to make everything look as fair as possible, to tell what is called the official truth, to present a version of the truth which contains about seventy-five per cent of the actual article. So long as a force gets a victory somehow, all the ugly facts are smoothed and varnished over, rotten reputations are propped up, and officers known as incapable are allowed to hang on and linger in their commands in the hope that at the end of the war they may be shunted into private life wihout a scandal.

During this speech Churchill argued in favour of 'the policy of candour'.[1] He was also developing a determined advocacy of the right of free speech. When a violent mob at Birmingham prevented Lloyd George from speaking at the Town Hall, Churchill wrote at once to the President of the Birmingham Conservative Association, J. Moore-Bayley: 'I hope the Conservative Party have kept their hands clean.'[2] And when the President sought to defend the just anger of Conservatives against Lloyd George's pro-Boer attitude, Churchill replied:

I think such methods equally disgraceful whether they are employed for or against the Conservative Party. You will find that the public opinion of the country will regard the whole episode as a blot upon the civilisation of Birmingham. If people say things which are treasonable and within the scope of the law they should be prosecuted and dealt with accordingly, but within the law every man has a perfect right to express his own opinions, and that they should be shouted down because they are odious to the majority in the district is a very dangerous, fatal doctrine for the Conservative Party, who may not always have the weight of numbers on their side to encourage. I shudder to think of the harm that would have been done to the Imperial cause in South Africa if Mr Lloyd George had been mauled or massacred by the mob. If your head clerk had made his presence known, he would have run a very great chance of being made answerable for the consequences. Personally, I think Lloyd George a

---

[1] House of Commons, 12 March 1901.
[2] Letter of 19 December 1901, *Churchill*, document volume 2, page 103.

vulgar, chattering little cad, but he will have gained a hundred thousand sympathisers in England by the late proceedings.

'We have all been very pleased', Churchill added, 'to see that in London the Conservative paper, the *Daily Graphic*, has clearly repudiated any sympathy with the outrage.'[1]

There was a second subject which Churchill raised in this letter to Moore-Bayley, a subject which was very soon to link him closely and sympathetically with Lloyd George. This was the question of social reform. It was a question to which Churchill had already alluded in the context of his criticisms of jingoism and excessive military spending. Now it was to move to the centre of his political philosophy, and quickly to become the driving force of more than a decade of argument and legislation.

The moment of transformation was a dinner at the Athenaeum. Churchill's host was the Liberal statesman, John Morley, and the turning-point came when Morley gave Churchill a newly published book on living conditions in York. As Churchill wrote twelve days later, to the Birmingham Conservative leader:

I have lately been reading a book by Mr Rowntree called *Poverty*, which has impressed me very much, and which I strongly recommend you to read. It is quite evident from the figures which he adduces that the American labourer is a stonger, larger, healthier, better fed, and consequently more efficient animal than a large proportion of our population, and that is surely a fact which our unbridled Imperialists, who have no thought but to pile up armaments, taxation and territory, should not lose sight of. For my own part, I see little glory in an Empire which can rule the waves and is unable to flush its sewers. The difficulty has been so far that the people who have looked abroad have paid no attention to domestic matters, and those who are centred on domestic matters regard the Empire merely as an encumbrance. What is wanted is a well-balanced policy midway between the Hotel Cecil and Exeter Hall, something that will co-ordinate development and expansion with the progress of social comfort and health. But I suppose the Party machinery will carry everything before it, and, as heretofore, the Extremists on both sides, whether progressive or reactionary, will set the tune and collar the organisation, and all we wretched,

[1] Letter of 23 December 1901, *Churchill*, document volume 2, page 104.

unorganised middle thinkers will either be destroyed between the contending forces, or compelled to serve in support of one disproportionate cause or the other.[1]

The influence on Churchill of Seebohm Rowntree's book was considerable. The high proportion of poor people in York was, Churchill believed, 'a rough measure of those in poverty throughout the cities of the land'. And in a book review of *Poverty* he wrote:

We indulge day dreams of fairy castles and bright hopes which can never be realised. We rejoice in the idea of Aladdin and his wonderful lamp. Desire lends force to fancy. Who has not considered how he would spend vast wealth? But from the ugly things of life, from its darker facts and hideous possibilities imagination recoils or is deliberately recalled. It is pleasureable to dwell upon the extremes of wealth. We do not wish to contemplate the extreme of poverty. The splendour of the palace, the glitter of the cavalcade, all the pomp & pageantry of life are familiar to enormous numbers of homely comfortable people: the slum, the garret & the gutter and strictly relegated by social arrangement & mental habit to their own peculiar limits.

Churchill ended his review of Rowntree's book with a passage full of anger, and charged with a fierce irony:

Consider the peculiar case of these poor, and the consequences. Although the British Empire is so large, they cannot find room to live in it; although it is so magnificent, they would have had a better chance of happiness if they had been born cannibal islanders of the Southern seas; although its science is so profound, they would have been more healthy if they had been subjects of Hardicanute. But it would be absurd to trust to such arguments, impudent to urge them upon a Parliament busy with matters so many thousand miles from home. There is a more important consideration. Not the duty of a man to man, nor the doctrines that honest effort in a wealthy community should involve certain minimum rights, nor that this festering life at home makes world wide power a mockery, and defaces the image of God upon earth. It is a serious hindrance to recruiting.

Let it be granted that nations exist and peoples labour to produce armies with which they conquer other nations, and the nation best qualified to do this is of course the most highly civilised and the most

---

[1] Letter of 23 December 1901, *Churchill*, document volume 2, page 104.

deserving of honour. But supposing the common people shall be so stunted and deformed in body as to be unfit to fill the ranks the army corps may lack. And thus—strange as it may seem, eccentric, almost incredible to write—our Imperial reputation is actually involved in their condition.

It is because I desire to contribute something to the recruiting problem that I would ask for a patient consideration for what is written. Of course it is a vy great nuisance that statesmen should have their minds diverted from the issues of war, diplomacy or colonization, to have to attend to such parochial matters, and I do not wonder that clever people write to the *Times* to show how much better it would be if the same sort of British legislative assembly were instituted to deal with local affairs and to provide the money while the Imperial senate concerned itself only with the high & important question of how to spend it. But in the present circumstances of the British Constitution— for which no loyal conservative can have any respect—we are unfortunately compelled to burden these great men with all sorts of business which affects these small islands; and therefore for the present and until we can make some arrangement, more suited to the spirit of the age, they must in some degree be held responsible if the manhood of the British nation deteriorates so much that she can no longer provide a status of recruits fit to fall in line with our colonial brothers.

One idea in this review was gradually to move to the centre of Churchill's thinking, 'that honest effort in a wealthy community should involve certain minimum rights'.[1] But it was not always easy to win support for this approach. Popular audiences, Churchill wrote to Lord Rosebery six months later, 'seem to gape for party clap trap'.[2] And it was the intensity of Party conflict which led Churchill, towards the end of his second year as a Conservative MP, to raise the idea of what he described to Lord Rosebery—a former Liberal Prime Minister—as 'a central coalition'. As Churchill explained to Rosebery:

The Government of the Middle—the party wh shall be free at once from the sordid selfishness & callousness of Toryism on the one hand & the blind appetites of the Radical masses on the other—may be an ideal wh we perhaps shall never attain, wh could in any case only be

[1] The full review is reprinted in *Churchill*, document volume 2, pages 105-11.
[2] Letter of 10 June 1902, Rosebery papers, printed in *Churchill*, document volume 2, page 146.

possessed for a time, but which is nevertheless worth working for: & I for my part, see no reason to despair of that 'good state'.

'The one real difficulty I have to encounter', Churchill reflected, 'is the suspicion that I am moved by mere restless ambition', but he added, 'if some definite issue—such as Tariff—were to arise—that difficulty would disappear'.[1]

The issue of Tariffs was indeed about to be revived, as Joseph Chamberlain sought to move the Conservative Party towards a new policy, aimed at Imperial unity, and based upon Protection. Churchill's instinct was already for Free Trade, of which he was, he informed his Constituents, a 'sober admirer'.[2] And in a letter to a Constituent who favoured Protection, he wrote:

> . . . it would seem to me a fantastic policy to endeavour to shut the British Empire up in a ringed fence. It is very large, and there are many good things which can be produced in it but the world is larger & produces some better things than can ever be found in the British Empire. Why should we deny ourselves the good and varied merchandise which the traffic of the world offers, more especially since the more we trade with others, the more they must trade with us; for it is quite clear that we give them something else back for everything they give to us. Our planet is not a very big one compared with the other celestial bodies, and I see no particular reason why we should endeavour to make inside our planet a smaller planet called the British Empire, cut off by impossible space from everything else. The idea does not attract me . . .[3]

Churchill again stressed the universal aspect of Free Trade in a letter to the leader of the Birmingham Conservatives:

> I do not want a selfcontained Empire. It is very much better that the great nations of the world should be interdependent one upon the other than that they should be independent of each other. That makes powerfully for peace and it is chiefly through the cause of the great traffic of one great nation with another during the last twenty five

---

[1] Letter of 10 October 1902, Rosebery papers, printed in *Churchill*, document volume 2, page 168.

[2] Letter of 28 October 1902, to the *Oldham Chronicle*, printed in *Churchill*, document volume 2, page 169.

[3] *Churchill*, document volume 2, pages 174-5.

years that the peace of Europe has been preserved through so many crises.

And even if it comes to an European war, do you not think it very much better that the United States should be vitally interested in keeping the English market open, than that they should be utterly careless of what happens to their present principal customer?[1]

By the early summer of 1903 Churchill had decided that if the Conservatives abandoned Free Trade, he would no longer remain a Conservative. Within twelve months, as the Tariff wing of the Party gained the ascendancy, he crossed the floor of the House of Commons, to sit on the Liberal benches. But although Free Trade was the issue, it was not the cause of his move. Every aspect of the Conservatism of 1903 distressed him. The clash between the Government and the Trade Unions was one example. As Churchill wrote to his mother:

The Trade Union matter is as you suppose tiresome & difficult. There is much reason in their case: yet they make unreasonable demands. These demands the Conservatives meet with flat refusal. I want to see them grapple with the difficulties & remove the force from the demand by conceding all that is just in it.

'But middle courses', Churchill added, 'are proverbially unpopular.'[2]

Ten months later, in a letter to *The Times*, Churchill commented: 'trade unionists will not be such fools as to hand themselves over to capitalist combinations at the very moment when, owing to the state of the law, they have lost much of the power and freedom which Lord Beaconsfield intended them to have.'[3]

Churchill's evolution from Conservative to Liberal was marked by a parallel development of his philosophy. Yet it is important to note that the ideas which he now began to expound to vast public audiences had already existed in embryo eight or nine years before, and were to remain at the centre of his beliefs both during his subsequent Ministerial life, and during

[1] Letter of 20 May 1903, *Churchill*, document volume 2, page 183.
[2] Letter to his mother, written in December 1902 for Assuan, *Churchill*, document volume 2, page 177.
[3] *The Times*, 12 October 1903.

his long periods of opposition and isolation. The Government, he told a correspondent in July 1903, 'must look to the well being of the country as a whole, not to that of any particular class or section'.[1] As to the best means of stimulating British commercial policy, he told another inquirer, 'I would look to improvements in scientific and technical education, to light taxation, to fiscal policy, and to a stable and orderly state of society.'[2]

Churchill was not yet formally a Liberal. In July 1903 he was still seeking support for his underlying idea 'of some sort of central government being formed',[3] and he was to revive this idea in 1910, at one of the most acrimonious moments in British political history. But in the autumn of 1903, in a letter which he wrote to one of his closest Conservative friends, but did not send, he explained why he would soon be making the definite change of Party:

I am an English Liberal. I hate the Tory party, their men, their words & their methods. I feel no sort of sympathy with them—except to my own people at Oldham. I want to take up a clear practical position which masses of people can understand. I do not want to stay splitting hairs upon retaliation and contracting all sorts of embarrass- ing obligations . . . .

To go on like this wavering between opposite courses, feigning friendship to a party where no friendship exists, & loyalty to leaders whose downfall is desired, sickens me. Moreover from a tactical point of view it is the surest road to destruction. . . .

The Tory party would show me no mercy, & I do not expect it or desire it. But upon the other hand I want to be free to defend myself— and I mean to be. It is therefore my intention that before Parliament meets my separation from the Tory party and the Government shall be complete & irrevocable; & during the next session I propose to act consistently with the Liberal party.

. . . Free Trade is so essentially Liberal in its sympathies & tendencies that those who fight for it must become Liberals. The duty of those who mean to maintain it is not to remain a snarling band on the flank of a

---

[1] Letter of 1 July 1903, to J. H. Lawton, *Churchill*, document volume 2, page 206.

[2] Letter of 9 July 1903, to Colonel J. Mitford, *Churchill*, document volume 2, page 208.

[3] Letter of 14 July 1903, to Sir J. Dickson-Poynder, *Churchill*, document volume 2, page 212.

government who mean to betray it, but boldly & honestly to range themselves in the ranks of that great party without whose instrumentality it cannot be preserved. . . .

It would be far better for the country in the long run if you were to face the real facts of the case and help to preserve a reconstituted Liberal party against the twin assaults of capital & Labour.

Thus Churchill became a Liberal; but he was under no illusions about the nature of Party politics, even among his new-found colleagues. The Liberal machine, he wrote to a Conservative friend on the eve of his conversion, 'seems to be just as stupid and brutalized as ours'.[1] His hope was to guide that machine, or at least those who directed it, more to his own viewpoint. In November 1903 he proposed to Lord Rosebery the setting up of a private committee of six or seven MPs to co-ordinate the entire Free Trade press, and to influence it 'from some central point of view'.[2]

Churchill did not move towards Liberalism alone. Some forty Conservative MPs, many of them young like himself, had joined the ranks of the Unionist Free Traders, and were poised uncertainly on the fringe of one party, and at the margin of another. But it was Churchill who first made the decisive move into the Liberal ranks. His day of truth came on 31 December 1903, a month after his twenty-ninth birthday, and the occasion was a private lunch with Lloyd George, the 'vulgar, chattering little cad' of two years before.

To Churchill's surprise, Lloyd George showed himself sympathetic to the plight of the Unionist Free Traders, and also in favour of Churchill's concept of a constructive social programme which could link the Unionist Free Traders and the Liberal Party in a common policy. As Churchill wrote to Lord Hugh Cecil:

Lloyd George spoke to me at length about a positive programme. He said unless we have something to promise as against Mr Chamberlain's promises where are we with the working men? He wants to promise

[1] Letter of 3 November 1903, to Lord Hugh Cecil, *Churchill*, document volume 2, page 249.
[2] Letter of 17 November 1903, Rosebery papers, quoted in *Churchill*, document volume 2, pages 252-3.

three things which are arranged to deal with three different classes, namely, fixity of tenure to tenant farmers subject to payment of rent and good husbandry: taxation of site values to reduce the rates in the towns: and of course something in the nature of Shackleton's Trade Disputes Bill for the Trade Unionists. . . .

I was very careful not to commit myself on any of these points and I chaffed him as being as big a plunderer as Joe. But *entre nous* I cannot pretend to have been shocked. Altogether it was a very pleasant and instructive talk and after all Lloyd George represents three things:— Wales, English Radicalism and Nonconformists, and they are not three things which politicians can overlook.

Within a year Churchill had become a leading advocate of the 'positive programme', and was to mould and enlarge it to his wider viewpoint. But in the political turmoil of the moment he still could see no real way of making it work. As he explained to Lord Hugh Cecil: 'The difficulties of the political situation depress me and it seems to me that whatever we may do at this next election, the Tory party will become permanently capitalist and Protectionist in character and the Liberal party will be smashed to pieces between organised capital on the one hand and organised labour on the other.'[1]

Nearly two decades were to pass before this was the actual fate of the Liberal Party. Meanwhile, it was to fall to Churchill, as much as to Lloyd George, to try to devise a Liberal policy capable of reflecting his now firm philosophical belief in the middle ground, the rights of the individual, and the responsibility of the State to preserve these rights, while acting as the impartial benefactor of those who were poor or unemployed. Hitherto, Churchill told his new Liberal constituents in the spring of 1904, his efforts had been in resisting Conservative Party tendencies 'towards militarism and monopoly'; now he would seek to guide British politics towards 'a higher regard for the rights of others', and 'a firmer reliance upon those moral forces of liberty and justice' that had made Britain renowned.[2]

Twice, before his formal crossing to the Liberal benches, Churchill indicated that he regarded these moral forces as

[1] Letter of 1 January 1904, Quickswood papers, published in *Churchill*, document volume 2, pages 281–5.
[2] *Manchester Courier*, 19 April 1904.

having equal weight abroad as at home. In March 1904, on learning of how Younghusband's expedition to Tibet 'had killed by machine gun fire six hundred Tibetan soldier-peasants at the village of Guru, for no British casualties', he wrote to Lord Hugh Cecil:

Surely it is vy wicked to do such things. Absolute contempt for the rights of others must be wrong. Are there any people in the world so mean-spirited as not to resist under the circumstances to which these poor Tibetans have been subjected. It has been their land for centuries, and although they are only Asiatics 'liberty' & 'home' mean something to them. That such an event should be greeted with a howl of ferocious triumph by Press & Party must be an evil portent.[1]

Within two months Churchill's anger had again been roused by a report on the terrible conditions for Negro workers in the mines of South Africa. He was indignant also at the claim by some Conservatives that this was not the proper province of Parliament, and by others that it was the Government's duty not to interfere with the policy of the companies concerned. In his last speech as a young Conservative, he told the House of Commons:

A good many people said that the House of Commons took too much interest in subjects of this kind, and that they were inclined to be carried away by humanitarian considerations. They were told that the people who were interesting themselves in this matter were hysterical and maudlin. Those who reprobated humanitarian sentiment in others were very often people who had never seen a man flogged or killed. But the responsibility of the House in these matters was very great. They exerted influence and authority over the affairs of more than 400,000,000 people. Every official, from the highest to the lowest, from the Viceroy to the smallest Jack-in-office, in the whole hierarchy of the British Empire was influenced by the standard which was upheld or lowered in that House. Therefore they were bound in all cases of cruelty and the invasion of the rights of subject races to be vigilant and emphasize these facts even if it meant interrupting the course of Parliamentary business and causing inconvenience. . . .

We must not only regard the financial interests of these prosperous

[1] Letter of 31 March 1904, Quickswood papers, printed in *Churchill*, document volume 2, page 328.

companies, but we must remember the human interest of the miner at the bottom of the mine.

He hoped it would establish clearly that in all the wide dominions of the King there was no man so unfortunate and so humble as to have his ill-treatment beneath the notice of that House, and that there was no province in the British Empire so distant as to be beyond their reach.[1]

[1] House of Commons, 5 May 1904.

II

RESPONSIBILITIES
1904-1924

On 31 May 1904 Churchill crossed the floor of the House of Commons, to take his seat as a Liberal. Henceforth, for twenty years, he was to be a leading advocate of Liberal policies; and for fifteen of those years he was to have one or other Government department through which to press his ideas and initiate legislation.[1] Henceforth, his political philosophy was to show itself not merely in public speeches or private letters, but in Parliamentary Acts and Departmental Regulations.

Churchill's first campaign from the Liberal benches was concerned, once more, with the rights of the individual: in this case not even the individual Briton, but the individual Jew. For on the very day that he sat for the first time on the Liberal benches, one of his attacks on the Conservative Government's Alien Bill was published in the *Manchester Guardian*. The new Bill, Churchill wrote, would not deter the professional thief, the anarchist, or the prostitute from entering Britain. Instead, he wrote, it was the 'simple immigrant, the political refugee, the helpless and the poor—these are the folk who will be caught in the trammels of the bill and may be harassed and hustled at the pleasure of petty officials without the smallest right of appeal to the broad justice of the English courts'. There were, Churchill insisted, no 'urgent or sufficient reasons, racial or social, for departing from the old tolerant and generous practice of free entry to which this country has so long adhered and from which it has so often greatly gained'.[2]

[1] He was successively Under-Secretary of State for the Colonies, President of the Board of Trade, Home Secretary, First Lord of the Admiralty, Chancellor of the Duchy of Lancaster, and (in Lloyd George's Coalition) Minister of Munitions, Secretary of State for War and Air, and Secretary of State for the Colonies.

[2] *Manchester Guardian*, 31 May 1904.

For the next year Churchill was to fight the Aliens Bill in the Press, on public platforms, and in Parliament. His criticisms of it in Committee stage were his first experience of the slow, detailed, and precise work required to challenge controversial legislation clause by clause. Nor did his concern cease after the Liberals, having been voted into office, allowed regulations similar to those in the Act to remain in force.

As Churchill wrote to Herbert Samuel, then Under-Secretary of State at the Home Office, and himself a Jew:

British citizenship is a privilege well worth an earnest effort to win. It is not and ought never to be a mere formality, but rather the solemn acceptance of duties & dignities. But I quarrel with our present regulations because they impose a wholly unreasonable & untrust-worthy test which capriciously disregards the merits & the character of the applicant, and bars only the poor. Five pounds ten shillings is a very serious disbursement for a working man however thrifty he may be, & to many men of good record & conduct, who have laboured industriously & have faithfully performed all the duties of a British citizen for many years, so great a sum is often in fact an absolute impediment. This is another instance of that same odious principle of a poverty test which we stigmatised in the Aliens Act, which accords the truest enfranchisement to a well-to-do person however undesirable he may be, & shuts the door with a slam in the face of a poor man however honestly & high-mindedly he may have lived. I am therefore strongly of opinion that whatever other tests may be prescribed, the naturalisation fee should be reduced. I think such a reform would come appropriately from a Liberal Government & with special grace from one who bears a name honoured throughout the world wherever counsels of sympathy & tolerance are in the ascendant.[1]

Churchill persevered in his efforts to reverse the Aliens Act, which, after his Jewish constituents had shown him details of its working, he described to the Home Secretary as a 'very harsh and quite indefensible measure'.[2] Thirty-five years later, with Hitler master of Europe, Churchill was to intervene again and again on behalf of Jewish refugees who had managed to escape. When, at the end of 1942, General Wavell warned of the

---

[1] Letter of 7 December 1906. *Churchill*, document volume 2, pages 604-5.
[2] Letter of 8 February 1907, *Churchill*, document volume 2, page 646.

dangers of Arab disorder if the two thousand survivors of the refugee ship *Patria* sunk in Haifa Bay, were allowed to remain in Palestine, Churchill informed the General: 'Personally, I hold it would be an act of inhumanity unworthy of British name to force them to re-embark.'[1]

Nearly two years later, when Lord Moyne expressed his concern about the problems involved ·in accepting a group of some fifty rich Jews who had bought their way out of Nazi-dominated Hungary, Churchill wrote to Anthony Eden: 'We should take a great responsibility if we prevented the escape of Jews, even if they should be rich Jews. I know it is the modern view that all rich people should be put to death whenever found, but it is a pity that we should take up that attitude at the present time. After all, they have no doubt paid for their liberation so high that in future they will only be poor Jews, and therefore have the ordinary rights of human beings.'[2]

It was these 'ordinary rights of human beings' that Churchill had championed across the intervening forty years.

In December 1905, at the age of thirty-one, Churchill entered the Government as Under Secretary of State for the Colonies, and for more than two years was responsible, under his Minister, Lord Elgin, for a wide spectrum of Colonial affairs. Even in the day-to-day detailed work of a Government department, his philosophy was evident. Reading in the files that a railway guard in Ceylon had be dismissed for inefficiency, after charges of theft had *failed* to be proven against him, Churchill wrote at once to the Governor of Ceylon to protest that the method of the guard's dismissal was 'to my mind a dangerous and undesirable procedure'.[3]

The Governor, irritated by Churchill's intervention, protested direct to Lord Elgin. But Churchill was emphatic that 'law and justice affecting a humble person' should be upheld, writing to Elgin:

[1] Telegram of 2 December 1942, quoted in Martin Gilbert, *Exile and Return*, London 1978, page 250.
[2] Letter of 14 July 1944, Prime Minister's Personal Minute, M 862/4, Churchill papers, 20/153.
[3] Letter of 27 August 1906, *Churchill*, document volume 2, page 575.

... let me say most solemnly that the Liberal party cares vy much for the rights of individuals to just & lawful treatment, & vy little for the petty pride of a Colonial Governor.

I can only say that a determination not to consent to such improprieties which are cruel to individuals & fatal to good Government has always actuated me, & that I will never depart from it because it is expedient in the supposed interests of discipline.[1]

A futher issue which showed the practical application of Churchill's philosophy of the rights of the individual was the Zulu revolt in Natal. During the summer of 1906 three thousand Zulus were killed, and four thousand taken prisoner. Churchill at once sought to restrain the Natal Government in their harsh treatment, telling Elgin: 'We cannot help unless we can also mitigate.'[2] In another minute to Elgin he argued that what he called 'the disgusting butchery of natives', and what he believed to be miscarriages of justice, revealed 'the kind of tyranny against which these unfortunate Zulus have been struggling'.[3]

Following the deportation of the leaders of the Zulu revolt to St. Helena, Churchill again sought to intervene, this time against the work and dietary conditions imposed by the Governor of the island. After studying the food scale he protested that it was more 'suited to the lowest animals than men',[4] and after reading the Governor's defence of his policy Churchill wrote to Elgin:

I do not like his tone at all. It is quite clear that he has no sympathy with these unfortunate men. We seem to have the spirit of Sir Hudson Lowe revived again in a most petty and prosaic form over these dusky captives. I do not look upon them as murderers, although no doubt that is their legal status. It has always been understood that they should be treated more like political *détenus* than common convicts. I do not think that the House of Commons would be impressed by their dietary. If they are to have no other groceries than salt, it is clear that their confinement will be most rigorous in this respect. I do not accept the easy assurance of the Governor that Zulus do not eat other groceries except salt, for I remember that he himself telegraphed to the

[1] Letter of 19 January 1907, *Churchill*, document volume 2, page 631.
[2] Minute of 16 January 1907, Colonial Office papers, 179/240/1138.
[3] Minute of 25 May 1907, Colonial Office papers, 179/241/18285.
[4] Minute of 24 July 1907, Colonial Office papers, 247/168/26220.

Government of Natal saying that the Zulu prisoners who were in St Helena some years ago were allowed to have any groceries they liked.

I do not think that stone-breaking ought to be their only employment. They ought to have a moderate task upon the roads each day; but after they have done their allotted task, they should be allowed to cultivate a small patch of land on which they could grow vegetables for their own use or for sale.

I do not see why they should not be taught to make baskets or carve wood, or make shoes, or some other simple form of light work, and I think that if any profit be made from the sale of these articles, the money should be given to them to buy any extra comforts they may wish.

I think that the Governor ought to be impressed by the fact that you are in earnest about the pledges which have been given to the House of Commons and that you will hold him responsible if he does not exert himself to make the lot of these unhappy Zulu exiles as little miserable as is compatible with their safe custody.[1]

Another example of Churchill's intervention in a question of individual rights was the removal of Chief Sekgoma, the Batawana chief, and his replacement by a more popular and much younger man. Refusing to accept his dismissal, Sekgoma had been put into detention. The High Commissioner of South Africa wished to deport him, to avoid general disturbance. Churchill was stirred to protest, writing to Lord Elgin:

We cannot imprison him or deport him without flat violation of every solid principle of British justice. As at present advised I could not undertake even to attempt a defence of the lawless deportation of an innocent man upon an informal *lettre de cachet*. If we are going to embark on this sort of law-breaking and autocratic action, where are we going to stop? What kind of injustice is there that would not be covered by precedents of this kind?

If we are going to take men who have committed no crime, and had no trial, and condemn them to life-long imprisonment and exile in the name of 'State policy' why stop there? Why not poison Sekgoma by some painless drug? No argument, that will justify his deportation to the Seychelles, will not also sustain his removal to a more sultry clime.

---

[1] Letter of 1 September 1907, Elgin papers, printed in *Churchill*, document volume 2, pages 666-7.

If we are to employ medieval processes, at least let us show medieval courage and thoroughness. Think of the expense that would be saved. A dose of laudanum, costing at the outside five shillings, is all that is required. There would be no cost of maintenance, no charges for transportation, no legal difficulties, no need to apply to the Portuguese, no fear of the habeas corpus. Without the smallest money or expense the peace of the Protectorate would be secured, and a 'dangerous character' obnoxious to the Government, removed.

If however, as I apprehend, Secretary of State would be averse to this procedure, the next best thing is to obey the law, and to act with ordinary morality, however inconvenient.[1]

Churchill gained no public credit for supporting the rights of a Ceylonese railway guard, of a Batawana chieftain, or of twenty-five Zulu deportees. The support he gave was offered behind the scenes, in the secrecy of Cabinet and Departmental exchanges. Yet here were the actual issues with which he had to deal as a junior minister, and in his response to them can be seen the workings of a political philosophy the fixed parameters of which were both humanitarian and democratic.

*   *   *

It was while he was still Under-Secretary of State at the Colonial Office that Churchill also began to develop his philosophy of the responsibility of the State towards the sick, the struggling, and the poor. It was a philosophy which was to lead him, as President of the Board of Trade in 1908, as Home Secretary in 1910, and as Chancellor of the Exchequer in 1924, to put on the Statute Book several lasting measures of social reform, and to contribute to the evolution of a fairer, and also a more tolerant, society.

Churchill had first set out his ideas in public when he spoke at Glasgow in the autumn of 1906, urging that it was the duty of the Liberal Party to embrace those whom he called 'the left-out millions', and to this end he envisaged the State 'embarking on various novel and adventurous experiments'. And he went on to explain:

I do not want to impair the vigour of competition, but we can do

[1] Minute of 23 October 1906, Colonial Office papers, 417/434/38258.

much to mitigate the consequences of failure. We want to draw a line below which we will not allow persons to live and labour yet above which they may compete with all the strength of their manhood. We do not want to pull down the structure of science and civilisation—but to spread a net over the abyss.[1]

Churchill also spoke out, while still at the Colonial Office, against wealth which had been acquired as a result of speculation in land. This was not, he realized, a subject on which it would be easy to legislate. As he told an audience in April 1907: 'We have to face all the resources of a great monopoly so ancient that it has become almost venerable.' And he went on to tell his listeners:

We have against us all the modern money power. We have to deal with the apathy and levity of all sections of the public. We have against us the political machinery of class and privilege represented by the Second Chamber in the State.

There are only two ways in which people can acquire wealth. There is production and there is plunder. Production is always beneficial. Plunder is always pernicious, and its proceeds are either monopolized by a few or consumed in the mere struggle for possession. We are here to range definitely on the side of production and to eliminate plunder as an element in our social system. The present land system hampers, hobbles and restricts industry. . . . We are resolved if we can to prevent any class from steadily absorbing under the shelter of the law the wealth in the creation of which they have borne no share, wealth which belongs not to them, but to the community, wealth which they can only secure by vexatious obstruction of social and economic progress, far more injurious and wasteful than can be measured by their inordinate gains.[2]

For nearly two years Churchill sought to evolve a practical idea for spreading this net. As he wrote to a senior official at the Board of Trade who had agreed to help him with facts and figures, 'if we were able to underpin the whole existing social security apparatus with a foundation of comparatively low-grade state safeguards, we should in the result obtain something

[1] Speech of 11 October 1906, reprinted in Winston S. Churchill, *Liberalism and the Social Problem*, London 1909.

[2] Speech at Drury Lane Theatre, London, 20 April 1907. Extracts in Churchill papers, 2/415.

that would combine the greatest merits both of the English and the German systems'. Churchill went on to explain that 'these ideas of minimum standards of life and wages, of security against going to the Devil through accident, sickness or weakness of character, and of competition upwards but not downwards', were to be the 'general theme' of a public speech later that month.[1]

In the spring of 1908 Churchill set out his ideas for specific social legislation in an article in *The Nation*. It was entitled 'The Untrodden Field in Politics', and as well as urging the end to such abuses, as he saw them, as the 'exploitation of boy labour', he also advocated State intervention over the whole field of employment and insurance, telling his readers:

Labour must be de-casualised by a system of Labour Exchanges. The resultant residuum must be curatively treated as if they were hospital patients. The hours of labour must be regulated in various trades subject to seasonal or cyclical fluctuations. Means must be found by which the State can, within certain limits and for short periods, augment the demand of the ordinary market for unskilled labour so as to counter-balance the oscillations of world trade. Underneath, though not in substitution for, the immense disjointed fabric of social safeguards and insurances which has grown up by itself in England, there must be spread—at a lower level—a sort of Germanised network of state intervention and regulation.[2]

In the year that followed the publication of this article, Churchill was to be at the centre of a major shift in the philosophy of liberalism and the legislation of the Liberal Government, now led by Asquith, who appointed Churchill to his first Cabinet post as President of the Board of Trade. As Churchill explained to Asquith, in accepting a Cabinet position in the domestic sphere:

Dimly across gulfs of ignorance I see the outline of a policy wh I call the Minimum Standard. It is national rather than departmental. I am

[1] Letter of 4 January 1908, to Arthur Wilson Fox, *Churchill*, document volume 2, page 759.

[2] *The Nation*, 7 March 1908. Churchill also advocated in this article the State acquisition of railways and canals.

doubtful of my power to give it concrete expression. If I did, I expect before long I should find myself in collision with some of my best friends—like for instance John Morley, who at the end of a lifetime of study & thought has come to the conclusion that nothing can be done.[1]

Churchill was determined that something should be done. Later he was to urge Asquith to consider such measures as unemployment and sickness insurance; State industries such as afforestation and road building, which could be deliberately expanded in times of unemployment; State control of the railways; and compulsory education until seventeen. 'I say', he told Asquith, 'thrust a big slice of Bismarckianism over the whole underside of our industrial system.'[2]

From Churchill's determination there emerged a series of Acts and Measures, including Labour Exchanges, the Trade Dispute Act, with its standing court of arbitration, the Trade Boards Act, which struck at the evil of sweated labour, and the preparation of a comprehensive scheme for compulsory contributory unemployment insurance, a scheme which Churchill worked out in detail, and which was then incorporated by Lloyd George as Part Two of the National Insurance Act of 1911. Defending one of the earliest of these measures, the Coal Mines (Eight Hours) Bill, Churchill told the House of Commons:

The general march of industrial democracy is not towards inadequate hours of work, but towards sufficient hours of leisure. That is the movement among the working people all over the country. They are not content that their lives should remain mere alternations between bed and the factory. They demand time to look about them, time to see their homes by daylight, to see their children, time to think and read and cultivate their gardens—time, in short, to live. That is very strange, perhaps, but that is the request they have made and are making with increasing force and reason as years pass by.

No one is to be pitied for having to work hard, for nature has contrived a special reward for the man who works hard. It gives him an extra relish, which enables him to gather in a brief space from simple pleasures a satisfaction in search of which the social idler wanders

[1] Letter of 14 March 1908, *Churchill*, document volume 2, page 755.
[2] Letter of 29 December 1908, *Churchill*, document volume 2, page 863.

vainly through the twenty-four hours. But this reward, so precious in itself, is snatched away from the man who has won it, if the hours of his labour be too severe to leave any time for him to enjoy what he has won.[1]

Churchill was under no illusions as to the extent of the social problem. 'Whilst our vanguard enjoys all the delights of all the ages', he told a Birmingham audience in January 1909, 'our rearguard struggles out into the conditions which are crueller than barbarism.' Yet wherever the reformer cast his eye, he was confronted 'with a mass of largely preventable and even curable suffering'.[2]

This was in no way mere rhetoric. Even as he spoke, Churchill was evolving practical schemes for presentation to Parliament. In the week before his Birmingham speech he had organized a series of Departmental Conferences at the Board of Trade, on Sweated Labour, Labour Exchanges, railway policy, and the centralization of electricity supply. As part of his attack on sweated labour, he had also put the finishing touches to a new conciliation procedure. Running through the new procedure, he explained in a private letter to Asquith, was 'the same idea which the Germans call *Paritätisch*—joint and equal representation of masters and men, plus the skilled permanent impartial element'.[3]

For Churchill, the principal fight against poverty lay in State-aided Insurance. As he told an audience at Manchester four months later:

If I had my way I would write the word 'Insure' over the door of every cottage, and upon the blotting-book of every public man, because I am convinced that by sacrifices which are inconceivably small, which are all within the power of the very poorest man in regular work, families can be secured against catastrophes which otherwise would smash them up for ever. I think it is our duty to use the strength and the resources of the State to arrest the ghastly waste not merely of human happiness but of national health and strength which follows when a working man's home which has taken him years to get together is

[1] House of Commons, 6 July 1908.

[2] Speech of 13 January 1909, reprinted in Winston S. Churchill, *Liberalism and the Social Problem*, London 1909.

[3] Letter of 12 January 1909, *Churchill*, document volume 2, page 870.

broken up and scattered through a long spell of unemployment, or when, through the death, the sickness, or the invalidity of the bread-winner, the frail boat in which the fortunes of the family are embarked founders, and the women and children are left to struggle helplessly on the dark waters of a friendless world.[1]

Three and a half months later Churchill told an audience at Leicester:

The greatest danger to the British empire and to the British people is not to be found among the enormous fleets and armies of the European Continent, nor in the solemn problems of Hindustan; it is not the Yellow peril nor the Black peril nor any danger in the wide circuit of colonial and foreign affairs. No, it is here in our midst, close at home, close at hand in the vast growing cities of England and Scotland, and in the dwindling and cramped villages of our denuded countryside. It is there you will find the seeds of Imperial ruin and national decay— the unnatural gap between rich and poor, the divorce of the people from the land, the want of proper discipline and training in our youth, the exploitation of boy labour, the physical degeneration which seems to follow so swiftly on civilised poverty, the awful jumbles of an obsolete Poor Law, the horrid havoc of the liquor traffic, the constant insecurity in the means of subsistence and employment which breaks the heart of many a sober, hard-working man, the absence of any established minimum standard of life and comfort among the workers, and, at the other end, the swift increase of vulgar, joyless luxury—here are the enemies of Britain. Beware lest they shatter the foundations of her power.[2]

The same principles that had guided Churchill at the Board of Trade were to be his guide when he went to the Home Office in 1910. Encouraged in his efforts by John Galsworthy, he embarked within a few weeks of his appointment on a substantial plan of prison reform. As Churchill wrote to the King, in explaining his early measures:

A new effort is to be made to prevent people being sent to gaol for petty offences & thus familiarised with the degrading surroundings of

---

[1] Speech of 23 May 1909, reprinted in Winston S. Churchill, *Liberalism and the Social Problem*, London 1909.

[2] Speech of 5 September 1909, reprinted in Winston S. Churchill, *Liberalism and the Social Problem*, London 1909.

Prison. The Probation of Offenders Act is to be strictly enjoined on magistrates all over the country. A bill is to be introduced to secure by law a period of grace for the payment of fines—(90,000 people go to prison each year in default of payment a third of whom could probably have found money if a few days grace were allowed)

Over 5000 lads between 16 & 21 are sent to prison every year for such offences as swearing, stone throwing, gaming, football in the streets. This is pure waste. Mr Churchill thinks a system of defaulters' drills might be instituted—not military (wh would reflect upon the possession of arms) but physical exercises, vy healthy, vy disagreeable; that this might be done at the Police Station; that the boy might do his ordinary work besides, & not be sent to prison unless incorrigible or really dishonest.

No lad between 16 & 21 ought to be sent to prison for mere punishment. Every sentence should be conceived with the object of pulling him together & bracing him for the world: it should be in fact disciplinary & educative rather than penal. . . .

In the prisons themselves Mr Churchill proposes to reduce solitary confinements to 1 month (instead of 9) for all except 'old lags' or as they are more decorously called 'recidivists'. Power is taken to pamper the suffragettes & the passive resisters. Further every quarter there will be either a concert or a lecture in each convict prison. These wretched people must have something to think about, & to break the long monotony. Some months ago the Somersetshire Light Infantry quartered at the Verne asked leave to send their band in to play once to the Dartmoor convicts. The effect produced was amazing

These immunising influences must not be neglected. The more strictly discipline is maintained, the more indulgences may follow on good behaviour. There are to be special provisions & regulations for aged convicts & for weak-minded convicts. Lastly the whole system of Ticket of Leave is to be overhauled & reorganised. . . .

All the existing Prisoners Aid Societies will be asked to send representatives to a Central Agency, wh will be semi-official (half charitable, half authoritative). This agency will study every convict's case separately: will distribute all the convicts between the different societies: will through these Societies endeavour to help them take their places again in honest life; & the police supervision will be entirely suspended except in refractory cases.[1]

---

[1] Letter of 21 July 1910, Royal Archives, reprinted in *Churchill*, document volume 2, pages 1189–90. Seventy years later, on 14 November 1980, the *Oxford Times* reported a recent speech by Mr Justice May, to the effect that 'socially inadequate people, such as

For several months Churchill worked to master and to expand the details of his plan. As he explained to Asquith in September 1910, the committal of 125,000 petty offenders for a fortnight or less was 'a terrible and purposeless waste of public money and human character', and would be brought to an end. Juvenile offenders would have 'some kind of physical training' rather than prison. 'I believe', Churchill added, 'there is no better cure for rowdyism than drill.' All imprisonment for debt would be brought to an end, a measure, which affected more than 10,000 annual imprisonments, and was aimed particularly to help the working class. As Churchill explained to Asquith:

The law at present is open to grave reproach of partiality as between rich and poor. Only workpeople are sent to prison for not paying their debts. Mr Hooley[1] thrives in opulent insolvency. A thoroughly vicious system of credit, based on no proper security, is spreading among the working classes throughout the country. Its consequences are injurious both to thrift and honesty. Touts and tallymen go round with ever greater frequency and press cheap jewelry, musical instruments, and many other non-necessary articles upon the workman, and still more upon the workman's wife in his absence. The weekly payments, enforceable by imprisonment, are a source of endless vexation and worry to the household, and often a cause of fierce quarrels; not infrequently the workman is taken from his work to prison (under our manmade laws) for his wife's debts, and often his family is kept by the parish while the State is revenging by imprisonment the injury of a private creditor.

Churchill's other proposals for prison reform included the introduction of the principle of 'time to pay' for offences involving either prison or a fine, the principle that no occasional offender ought to be sent to prison 'for a single trivial offence', that all prison sentences of less than a month should henceforth be declared 'suspensory', and above all the classification of prisons according to a definite plan whereby the different institutions would be adopted 'to the suitable treatment of every

drunks and petty offenders, were unsuited to prison. However much of a nuisance they were to others, it did them no good to be imprisoned.'

[1] Ernest Hooley, a notorious stockbroker made bankrupt in 1898. In 1922 he was sentenced to three years' penal servitude for fraud. He died in 1947 at the age of 88.

conceivable variety of human weakness and misdemeanour'. Churchill also urged the need and possibility for a special Classification Board to allocate 'the appropriate treatment' to all offenders after sentence.[1]

These efforts at prison reform were very much a part of Churchill's political and social philosophy. They did not, however, go unchallenged in Parliament, where many Conservatives rejected his emphasis on care and regeneration. In defending his policies Churchill put them in their wider philosophical context, telling the House of Commons:

> The mood and temper of the public in regard to the treatment of crime and criminals is one of the most unfailing tests of the civilization of any country. A calm and dispassionate recognition of the rights of the accused against the State, and even of convicted criminals against the State, a constant heart-searching by all charged with the duty of punishment, a desire and eagerness to rehabilitate in the world of industry all those who have paid their dues in the hard coinage of punishment, tireless efforts towards the discovery of curative and regenerating processes, and an unfaltering faith that there is a treasure, if you can only find it, in the heart of every man—these are the symbols which in the treatment of crime and criminals mark and measure the stored-up strength of a nation, and are the sign and proof of the living virtue in it.[2]

Churchill's ideas, speeches, and legislative work between 1908 and 1910 helped to launch a revolution in the social philosophy of Britain; a bloodless revolution of substantial reforms inside the existing social structure. As such it was his aim to reform what was bad and to preserve what was good in Society, by evolution and fair dealing.

Churchill never abandoned his philosophy of the middle course. Even when leading the Liberal Government's challenge to the veto powers of the House of Lords, he still, while one of the fiercer critics of those powers, searched for the evolutionary rather than the revolutionary course. 'After the veto has been restricted', he wrote to Asquith at the height of the controversy, 'I hope we may be able to pursue *une politique d'apaisement.*' As

---

[1] Letter of 26 September 1910, *Churchill*, document volume 2, pages 1198–1203.
[2] House of Commons, 20 July 1910.

soon as the power of the Peers had been restricted, he added, 'You will be strong enough to pursue a sober and earnest policy without the stimulus of undue partisanship.'[1]

Churchill was always conscious of this ideal: the avoidance of 'undue partisanship'. Thus, during the early days of the South Wales riots, he wrote to the King: 'The owners are very unreasonable as well as the men, and both sides are fighting one another regardless of human interests or the public welfare.'[2] Later, during the Tonypandy riots, he ordered the troops who were then on their way from London, to be halted at Swindon, and replaced instead by unarmed policemen. Attacked by the Conservative Press for undue caution, Churchill told the House of Commons:

Law and order must be preserved, but I am confident that the House will agree with me that it is a great object of public policy to avoid a collision between soldiers and crowds of persons engaged in industrial disputes. . . . For soldiers to fire on the people would be a catastrophe in our national life. Alone among the nations, or almost alone, we have avoided for a great many years that melancholy and unnatural experience. And it is well worth while, I venture to think, for the Minister who is responsible to run some risk of broken heads or broken windows . . . to accept direct responsibility in order that the shedding of British blood by British soldiers may be averted, as, thank God, it has been successfully averted in South Wales.[2]

That autumn, during the Liverpool riots, Churchill did order troops to intervene to protect life and property. But their orders were clear: to fire only over the heads of the mob, and this they did. There were no deaths in Liverpool, although later still, at Llanelly, two men died after troops opened fire on a mob which had refused to disperse, after having halted and looted a train, and beaten the engineer unconscious.

Churchill deplored these deaths, which took place during severe rioting, looting, and lawlessness. But he was emphatic in his refusal to use troops during purely industrial disputes, telling

[1] Letter of 3 January 1911, *Churchill*, document volume 2, page 1032.
[2] Letter of 23 November 1910, Royal Archives, *Churchill*, document volume 2, page 1213.
[3] House of Commons, 7 February 1911.

the House of Commons in August 1911: 'There can be no question of the military forces of the crown intervening in a labour dispute.'[1]

Towards the miners themselves, Churchill sought a fair deal. He had already warned the mine owners not to expect the police or the army to act as 'their private lackeys and flunkeys'.[2] And in a long secret letter to Lloyd George in the spring of 1911 he explained his wish to improve the safety regulations in the mines, in order to meet the requests of the miners, who had been victims in 1910 of the highest death-rate through accidents since mining statistics had begun. New regulations, and more money for the Inspectorate, were essential, Churchill added, 'to stop this awful waste of human life', and in order to raise the money, he suggested 'a special surcharge' on the mine-owners' royalties. By such means, Churchill added, the Government could 'come to the rescue of this great community of labouring men'.[3]

Fifteen years later, Churchill was again to seek a fair deal for the miners in the aftermath of the General Strike, and was to go so far, to the distress of many of his Conservative colleagues, to seek to force the mine-owners to accept a uniform national minimum wage. Indeed, as Chancellor of the Exchequer at a time when unemployment was well over a million, he devoted five years to seeking the means of helping productive industry, and reducing industrial distress.

In his first Budget, introduced in April 1925, Churchill sought precise expression for his ideas. As a result of his measures, more than 200,000 widows and 350,000 orphans received immediate benefits while the pensionable age was lowered from 70 to 65 years. 'Restrictions, inquisitions and means tests', as Churchill described them, were abolished, while for all those in receipt of the new benefits, henceforth, Churchill insisted, 'it would be nobody's business what they had or how they employed their time'. Churchill explained these measures to the House of Commons:

I cherish the hope, Sir, that by liberating the production of new

[1] House of Commons, 15 August 1911.
[2] Quoted in A. P. Herbert, 'Winston and the Workers', in the *Spectator*, 28 June 1963.
[3] Letter of 3 March 1911, *Churchill*, document volume 2, pages 1247–8.

wealth from some of the shackles of taxation the Budget may stimulate enterprise and accelerate industrial revival, and that by giving a far greater measure of security to the mass of wage-earners, their wives and children, it may promote contentment and stability, and make our Island more truly a home for all these people.

Churchill's first Budget also contained an extension of State-supported health insurance to cover a total of 15 million wage-earners and 15 million dependants. 'Here, then', Churchill argued, 'is where the State, with its long and stable finance, with its carefully guaranteed credit, can march in to fill the immense gap.' And he stressed in particular the Government's duty to provide 'extra reward and indulgence' in order to help those who had been stricken by circumstances beyond their control. 'It is the stragglers, the exhausted, the weak, the wounded, the veterans, the widows and orphans', he declared, 'to whom the ambulances of State aid should be directed.'

Churchill's instinct for social justice was also shown in his first Budget by income-tax reductions which gave their greatest benefits to the lower-income groups (a 10 per cent reduction for earned incomes up to £2,000), as well as a scale of allowances designed to help the less well off. His aim, he said, was to 'stimulate enterprise and accelerate industrial revival' by, as he phrased it, 'liberating the production of new wealth from some of the shackles of taxation'.[1]

In defending his social reforms before a critical Conservative audience, the British Banker's Association, Churchill declared that his aim was to find an economic policy that would help 'every class and every section', and he added

That is our aim. The appeasement of class bitterness, the promotion of a spirit of co-operation, the stabilisation of our national life, the building of the financial and social plans upon a three or four years' basis instead of a few months basis, an earnest effort to give the country some period of recuperation after the enormous efforts it has made and the vicissitudes to which it has been subjected . . .[2]

*   *   *

[1] House of Commons, 28 April 1925.
[2] Speech of 13 May 1925, Gilbert, *Churchill*, volume 5, page 120.

Churchill's philosophy of wealth led him, while Chancellor of the Exchequer, to propose a series of taxes on unearned income and luxury goods, as well as on capital. As he himself expressed it: 'The process of the creation of new wealth is beneficial to the whole community. The process of squatting on old wealth though valuable is a far less lively agent.'

As Chancellor, Churchill was constantly proposing plans to stimulate 'the energetic creation of new wealth', arguing that 'a premium on effort is the aim, and a penalty on inertia may well be its companion'.[1]

*   *   *

Throughout the nine-day drama of the General Strike, Churchill played only a secondary part. In the Cabinet which broke off negotiations with the TUC, it was Baldwin who took the lead in opposing what all his colleagues believed to be an unconstitutional attempt to undermine Parliamentary democracy. The story current at the time in Labour circles of a 'war party' led by Churchill and (of all people) Neville Chamberlain was a myth. Equally mythical was Churchill's alleged dispatch of troops against the strikers.

Not Churchill, but a special Cabinet Committee of which he was not even a member, discussed and ordered the various strike-breaking measures from day to day. It was this Committee, headed by the Home Secretary, which asked Churchill to supervise the production of a Government newspaper, a task which he undertook with zeal, helped by a large journalistic staff, including a full-time editor.

This paper, the *British Gazette*, published Government speeches and statements, and news of the progress of the strike. 'I do not contemplate violent partisanship,' Churchill told the newspaper owners who gave their support in men, machines, and paper, 'but fair, strong encouragement to the great mass of loyal people.'[2] And in a series of unsigned articles in the paper itself he stressed, as the strike continued, that the Government

---

[1] For Churchill's letters and memoranda while Chancellor of the Exchequer see *Churchill*, document volume 5, 'The Exchequer Years', pages 246–1467, and Gilbert, *Churchill*, volume 5, pages 65–329.

[2] *Churchill*, document volume 5, 'The Exchequer Years', pages 693–700.

did not and ought not to rely on force, but 'on reason, on public opinion and on the will of the people'. It was essential, he added, never to forget, 'even in the heat and height of this struggle, that we are all fellow citizens'.[1]

This conciliatory tone was reflected in Churchill's speech in the House of Commons as the strike intensified. 'The door is always open', he declared. 'There is no question of there being a gulf across which no negotiator can pass—certainly not—it is our duty to parly.'[2] And Baldwin echoed these very phrases when he spoke two days later. Baldwin also warned, and the *British Gazette* gave prominence to his warning, that the General Strike was 'a challenge to Parliament' as well as 'the road to anarchy and ruin'.[3] Churchill himself, in another of his unsigned articles, told his readers: 'Every man and woman can do something to convince the strikers of the error and peril of their actions. It is far better that this should be accomplished by waves of public opinion than by other measures.'[4]

As the strikers moved towards collapse, Churchill wrote to Baldwin: 'Tonight surrender. Tomorrow magnanimity.' And he added: 'On the interval between these two depends the whole result of this deep conflict.'[5]

On the day the strike ended, the General Secretary of the TUC watched Churchill and Baldwin talking together at No. 10. 'There was no sign of jubilation', he noted. Churchill himself, while at No. 10, went up to Arthur Pugh (General Secretary of the Iron and Steel Trades Federation) with the words: 'Thank God it is over, Mr. Pugh.'[6]

The moment the General Strike ended, Churchill became, at Baldwin's personal request, the principal Government mediator in seeking to resolve the continuing Coal Strike, out of which the General Strike had arisen. For nearly five months Churchill used all his authority as Chancellor, and all his persuasive

---

[1] *Churchill*, document volume 5, 'The Exchequer Years', pages 703-7.

[2] House of Commons, 3 May 1926.

[3] *British Gazette*, 5 May 1926.

[4] *Churchill*, document volume 5, 'The Exchequer Years', pages 710-11.

[5] Letters of 11 May 1926, quoted in *Churchill*, document volume 5, 'The Exchequer Years', pages 716-17.

[6] Walter Citrine, *Men and Work: An Autobiography.*

powers, to put pressure on both owners and miners to reach a reasonable settlement. At one stage he went so far as to threaten legislation to force the mine-owners to accept the miners' basic demand for a uniform national minimum wage. But at the last hurdle, Churchill's Cabinet colleagues baulked at coercing the owners by means of legislation.

In one attempt to force the owners into a corner, Churchill held two secret meetings—one at Chartwell and one in London—with Ramsay MacDonald and the TUC leaders, in order to include, in the Government's own ultimatum to the mine-owners, exactly those terms acceptable to the Labour Party and the Unions.[1]

During these negotiations, Churchill opposed any curtailment (as wished by several Cabinet members) of the right of peaceful picketing. Nor would he countenance legislation to make a strike illegal if, as he put it, 'a majority of those affected were in favour of it'. He was emphatic also in using Government money, not to subsidize the owners, but to provide houses in mining areas, and 'for training schemes and other forms of assistance for displaced miners'.

Discussing the Government's proposed strike legislation, leading employers opposed even a secret ballot, arguing that it would lead to an increase in the number of strikes. Churchill disagreed, telling a special Cabinet Committee that he was 'convinced that the majority of working men would adopt a sound and sensible attitude'. The only effect of a secret ballot, he argued would be to restrict the influence of 'extremist members' of the Union.

Throughout the Coal negotiations Churchill was critical of what he called 'the greedy appetites of the coal trade', and when his cousin Lord Londonderry (himself a coal-owner) rebuked Churchill for not seeing that the mine-owners were 'fighting Socialism', Churchill replied: 'It is not the business of Coal Owners as Coal Owners to fight Socialism. If they declare it their duty, how can they blame the Miners Federation for

[1] Churchill's efforts and opinions during the Coal negotiations of 1926, as summarized here, can be followed in detail in *Churchill*, document volume 5, 'The Exchequer Years', pages 748–883.

pursuing political ends.' The business of the coal-owners, he added, 'is to manage their business successfully'.[1]

Churchill's experiences as Chancellor of the Exchequer between 1924 and 1929, and in particular his clashes with the mine-owners, and the Treasury mandarins, served to sharpen his political philosophy in the bordering realms of financial and economic policy. Ever since his doubts about the return to the Gold Standard had been overruled early in 1925, he had continued to argue with his senior officials that both the Treasury and the Bank of England had erred throughout the previous decade in having 'favoured finance at the expense of production'. In a letter to one of his senior advisers in January 1927, commenting on the Treasury view that the most recent increase in the national debt was 'an imaginary evil', Churchill warned that not only would the money have to be 'paid by our children and raised by taxation from *them*', but that 'the dead hand of the debt' would continue to rest for a longer period 'upon the productive energies of the country'. Of course, Churchill added, it was natural that the 'capitalists' interests' and the 'banking classes' should welcome a policy which, in his words, 'tends to foster to its highest point the interests of creditors and inert citizens of all kinds, at the expense of all those forces which by fresh efforts are perennially replacing what is consumed'.

Churchill accepted that the interests of the Bankers, the financial middlemen, and the 'Money Trust' could not be ignored. But he warned against raising these interests above the 'social, moral and manufacturing' aspects of national life. 'After all,' he wrote, 'there is more in the life of a nation than the development of an immense *rentier* class quartered in perpetuity upon the struggling producer of new wealth.'[2]

For Churchill, productivity was the key. 'Cultured people', he later remarked, 'are but the glittering scum on the deep river of production.'[3] It was thus to the producer and manufacturer

---

[1] Letter of 3 November 1926, Gilbert, *Churchill*, volume 5, pages 217–18.

[2] Letter of 26 January 1927, quoted in full in *Churchill*, document volume 5, 'The Exchequer Years', pages 924–6.

[3] Randolph Churchill diary, 24 August 1929, quoted in Randolph S. Churchill, *Twenty-One Years*, page 74.

that Churchill looked for the revival of the economy throughout his five years as Chancellor of the Exchequer.

*   *   *

War against Germany was twice to dominate Churchill's career, first in his early forties, as First Lord of the Admiralty and then Minister of Munitions, and again in his late sixties, as Prime Minister. Between the two wars he was to expand enormous mental energy on the question of foreign affairs and defence. Even before the First World War, while President of the Board of Trade, and in the midst of social reforms and social legislation, he had seen, as a guest of the Kaiser at German manœuvres, something of the scale and nature of the German army. Nor was his reaction militaristic. A decade had passed since he himself had been under fire. But as he wrote to his wife from Würzburg in 1909:

> This army is a terrible engine. It marches sometimes 35 miles in a day. It is in number as the sands of the sea—& with all the modern conveniences. There is a complete divorce between the two sides of German life—the Imperialists & the Socialists. Nothing unites them. They are two different nations.
>
> With us there are so many shades. Here it is all black & white (the Prussian colours). I think another 50 years will see a wiser & a gentler world. But we shall not be spectators of it. Only the P.K.[1] will glitter in a happier scene. How easily men could make things much better than they are—if they only all tried together! Much as war attracts me & fascinates my mind with its tremendous situations—I feel more deeply every year—& can measure the feeling here in the midst of arms— what vile & wicked folly & barbarism it all is.[2]

Within two years it was a German action which had brought Churchill into a new sphere. Just as, in 1901, he had been alerted to the full extent of social distress by Seebohm Rowntree's book on York, and had devoted the next decade to personal efforts to relieve that distress, so, in 1911, it was the Agadir crisis which focused his mind on foreign policy and defence.

---

[1] 'Puppy-Kitten': their daughter Diana, who had been born two months earlier.

[2] Letter of 15 September 1909, Spencer-Churchill papers, quoted in full in *Churchill*, document volume 2, pages 910–12.

Henceforth, Churchill was to link Britain's domestic prosperity, and indeed survival, with the country's ability not only
to defend itself, but to act as a pacific influence in world affairs,
and to be capable where necessary of decisive action to deter, or
to counter, aggression.

As the Agadir crisis proceeded, and in its aftermath,
Churchill sought to bring the whole question of defence within
the ambit of his political philosophy. Its first impact on him was
the extent of national unity when confronted with an external
threat. As he wrote to the King about the Parliamentary
response to Lloyd George's Mansion House speech, warning
Germany not to underestimate Britain's support for France:

> A great moment in the House of Commons, showing at its very best
> the power & dignity of this country. The Prime Minister made his
> statement—careful, & friendly in form & feeling, but strong & firm in
> substance. Then Mr Balfour—admirable, also vy short. No party
> dissensions even at their worst could affect national unity in great
> issues. Lastly Mr Ramsay Macdonald—restrained, sombre but per-
> fectly correct. The whole three speeches together occupying less than
> half an hour—in a dead hush with occasional deep murmurs of assent.
>
> No one else rose—the whole subject dropped & after a long pause a
> young Conservative member began to talk about Persia. It may well
> be that this episode following upon the speech of the Chancellor of
> the Exchequer will have exercised a decisive effect upon the peace
> of Europe. It is certain that it redounds to the credit of British public
> life.[1]

The second impact of Agadir on Churchill's thinking was the
link between foreign policy and defence preparations. As Home
Secretary he was, he discovered, responsible for the safety of the
two naval magazines in London, both of which had been left
undefended. He at once sent policemen to defend them, and
then persuaded the War Office to send soldiers. It was a small
incident, but its effect on his thinking was to be considerable.[2]

The third impact of Agadir on Churchill was his belief that
aggression could be deterred if the threatened States were to act
in unison. As in 1936, so in 1911, he saw the alliance of

---

[1] Letter of 27 July 1911, *Churchill*, document volume 2, page 1104.
[2] See Winson S. Churchill, *The World Crisis*, volume 1, pages 50-2.

threatened States not as an instrument of war, but as a means of preventing war, while at the same time wanting the arrangement of the alliance to be such that the war plans were real, and the deterrent credible. He first outlined these ideas in a letter to Sir Edward Grey, the Foreign Secretary, during the final phases of the Agadir crisis itself:

> Propose to France and Russia triple alliance to safeguard (*inter alia*) the independence of Belgium, Holland and Denmark.
>
> Tell Belgium that, if her neutrality is violated, we are prepared to come to her aid and to make an alliance with France and Russia to guarantee her independence. Tell her that we will take whatever military steps will be most effective for that purpose. But the Belgian Army must take the field in concert with the British and French Armies, and Belgium must immediately garrison properly Liège and Namur. Otherwise we cannot be responsible for her fate.
>
> Offer the same guarantee both to Holland and to Denmark contingent upon their making the utmost exertions.
>
> We should, if necessary, aid Belgium to defend Antwerp and to feed that fortress and any army based on it. We should be prepared at the proper moment to put extreme pressure on the Dutch to keep the Scheldt open for *all* purposes. If the Dutch close the Scheldt, we should retaliate by a blockade of the Rhine. . . .[1]

The fourth area of reflection prompted by Agadir was the question of *casus belli*. It was here that Churchill now looked at the concept of the dominance of Europe by a single power, by means of upsetting the balance of power in Europe, to Britain's detriment. As he wrote to Lloyd George: 'It is not for Morocco, nor indeed for Belgium, that I wd take part in this terrible business. One cause alone cd justify our participation—to prevent France from being trampled down & looted by the Prussian junkers—a disaster ruinous to the world, & swiftly fatal to our country.'[2]

Churchill had entered upon that phase of his thought which was to produce, over the coming thirty years, his most significant contributions to British attitudes and behaviour. The change was accentuated two months after Agadir, when

---

[1] Letter of 30 August 1911, *Churchill*, document volume 2, pages 1116-17.
[2] Letter of 31 August 1911, *Churchill*, document volume 2, page 1119.

Churchill was appointed First Lord of the Admiralty. Defence, and preparation for war, now became his official task. But in carrying it out he was also actively seeking a properly regulated measure of naval disarmament, the so called Naval Holiday, aimed at reducing tensions between Britain and Germany. And on the very eve of war he wrote to his wife: 'No one can measure the consequences. I wondered whether those stupid Kings and Emperors could not assemble together, and revivfy kingship, by saving the nations from Hell. But we all drift on in a kind of dull cataleptic trance. As if it were somebody else's operation.'[1]

During the war itself Churchill cast about for a means of shortening its duration, and of ending the cruelties of what he described as 'sending our armies to chew barbed wire in Flanders'.[2] His first idea was the Tank, his second, the Dardanelles. Neither idea shortened the war; the second, the Dardanelles, appeared effectively to shorten Churchill's career, if not to end it.[3] Nevertheless, as he wrote to his wife from the trenches on the Western Front, where he went to serve as a battalion commander: 'My conviction that the greatest of my work is still to be done is strong within me, and I ride reposefully along the gale.'[4] A month later, from his battalion headquarters in the line, he wrote again: 'I am impotent to give what there is to be given—of truth and value and urgency.' Six o'clock in the evening, he added, 'is a bad hour for me. I feel the need of power as an outlet worst then, and the energy of mind and body is strong within me.'[5]

Returning from the trenches, Churchill emerged as a leading Parliamentary opponent of the war of attrition, and he told the House: 'I say to myself every day, what is going on while we sit here, while we go away to dinner or home to bed? Nearly 1,000 men—Englishmen, Britishers, men of our own race—are knocked into bundles of bloody rags every twenty-four hours,

---

[1] Letter of 28 July 1914, *Churchill*, document volume 2, page 1989.

[2] Letter of 29 December 1914, *Churchill*, document volume 3, pages 343-5.

[3] For Churchill's account of his involvement in the genesis of the Tank see *Churchill*, document volume 4, pages 886-93; for a full account of the genesis and evolution of the Dardanelles campaign see Gilbert, *Churchill*, volume 3.

[4] Letter of 15 December 1915, *Churchill*, document volume 3, pages 1330-1.

[5] Letter of 19 January 1916, *Churchill*, document volume 3, pages 1383-4.

and carried away to hasty graves or to field ambulances . . .'[1] In the course of his speech Churchill spoke with sympathy of the men at the front: 'the men' he said, 'who pay all the penalties in the terrible ordeal which is now proceeding'.[2] And as Lloyd George gave his final authority for the capture of the Passchendaele ridge, Churchill told the House of Commons that his opposition was total to 'those dismal processes of waste and slaughter which are called attrition'.[3] After Passchendaele, Churchill wrote to a friend: 'Thank God our offensives are at an end. Let them make the pockets. Let them traipse across the crater fields. Let them rejoice in the occasional capture of placeless names & sterile ridges.'[4]

*   *   *

In July 1917 Churchill rejoined the Government as Minister of Munitions, and held this responsible post until the end of the war. Even in this quasi-military department, his sympathy was with those who made the weapons of war, not with those who might profit from them. As he wrote to a member of the War Cabinet:

Demands of the workers for increases of wages are not, in my opinion, disproportionate to what is natural and reasonable in all the circumstances of the present situation, and certainly they are not in excess of the increases either in the cost of living or in the degree of effort which has been forthcoming . . .[5]

As to war profiteering, his attitude was equally emphatic: 'The idea that any class has a right to make an excess profit out of the war', he told the War Cabinet,

must be combated wherever it appears and by every means open to the State. Under the existing law four-fifths of the excess profits are taken by taxation. It is impossible to rest satisfied with this provision, and

---

[1] House of Commons, 23 May 1916.

[2] House of Commons, 24 July 1916.

[3] House of Commons, 5 March 1917.

[4] Letter of 29 December 1917, to Sir Archibald Sinclair, printed in full in *Churchill*, document volume 4, pages 222–3.

[5] Letter of 10 November 1917, to Lord Milner, *Churchill*, document volume 4, page 195.

every practicable means will be employed by the Government to secure to the service of the country all excess profits made during this time of suffering.[1]

Churchill's work as Minister of Munitions involved him in having to deal with a series of strikes, some potentially disastrous for the war effort. But by means of face-to-face negotiations with the union leaders and conciliation, dislocation of industry was averted, and Churchill's faith in British common sense and sense of purpose was enhanced. 'Ask what you please,' he told the House of Commons after the German spring offensive of 1918, 'look where you will, you cannot get to the bottom of the resources of Britain. No demand is too novel or too sudden to be met. No need is too unexpected to be supplied. No strain is too prolonged for the patience of our people. No suffering or peril daunt their hearts.'[2]

*   *   *

The impact of the First World War on Churchill had been considerable. 'The war weighs heavy on us all', he wrote to a friend in the spring of 1917, 'and amid such universal misfortune and with death so ubiquitous and life so harsh, I find a difficulty in setting pen to paper.'[3] Early in 1918, after a visit to the Ypres salient, he wrote to his wife: 'Nearly 800,000 of our British race have shed their blood or lost their lives here during $3\frac{1}{2}$ years of unceasing conflict. Many of our friends and my contemporaries all perished here. Death seems as commonplace and as little alarming as the undertaker. Quite a natural ordinary event, which may happen to anyone at any moment, as it happened to all these scores of thousands who lie together in this vast cemetery, ennobled and rendered forever glorious by their brave memory.'[4]

Part of the 'brave memory' which Churchill was later to recall with pride concerned the actual behaviour of the troops under stress. As he told the House of Commons in the summer of 1920:

[1] Memorandum of 31 December 1917, *Churchill*, document volume 4, pages 224-6.
[2] House of Commons, 25 April 1918.
[3] Letter to Sir Archibald Sinclair, 22 March 1917, *Churchill*, document volume 4, page 45.
[4] Letter of 23 February 1918, *Churchill*, document volume 4, pages 251-3.

Over and over again we have seen British officers and soldiers storm entrenchments under the heaviest fire, with half their number shot down before they entered the position of the enemy, the certainty of a long, bloody day before them, a tremendous bombardment crashing all around—we have seen them in these circumstances taking out their maps and watches, and adjusting their calculations with the most minute detail, and we have seen them show, not merely mercy, but kindness, to prisoners, observing restraint in the treatment of them, punishing those who deserved to be punished by the hard laws of war, and sparing those who might claim to be admitted to the clemency of the conqueror.

We have seen them exerting themselves to show pity and to help, even at their own peril, the wounded. They have done it thousands of times . . .[1]

Between 1919 and 1929 Churchill himself published six volumes of war history, entitled *The World Crisis*. As he wrote, he drew not only from his own experiences, but from the myriad war books of the time. These confirmed his belief in individual bravery and decency, as well as in the indecency of war itself. As he wrote to his wife, about one such book: 'If it is monotonous in its tale of horror, it is because war is full of inexhaustible horrors. We shall certainly never see the like again. The wars of the future will be civil and social wars, with a complete outfit of terrors of their own.'[2]

Churchill also understood the public desire for peace, and at the time of the Russo-Polish war, he wrote in the *Evening News*, of the British people: 'They are thoroughly tired of war. They have learnt during five bitter years too much of its iron slavery, its squalor, its mocking disappointments, its ever dwelling sense of loss.'[3]

Nine years later his own third volume of *The World Crisis* was published. The descriptions of the war on the Western Front, and of the Passchendaele offensive, constituted, wrote Keynes, 'a tractate against war—more effective than the work of a pacifist would be'.[4]

[1] House of Commons, 8 July 1920.
[2] Letter of 27 March 1920, *Churchill*, document volume 4, pages 1057-9. The book was *The Realities of War*, by Philip Gibbs.
[3] Article in the *Evening News*, 28 July 1920.
[4] *The Nation*, 5 March 1927.

Quoting Robertson's letter to Haig of 27 September 1917: 'I confess I stick to it more because I see nothing better, and because my instinct prompts me to stick to it, than because any good arguments by which I can support it', Churchill commented: 'These are terrible words when used to sustain the sacrifice of nearly four hundred thousand men.'[1]

The war itself, Churchill believed, was one between 'right and wrong'. But once the Germans were defeated, they must be treated 'with wisdom and justice'. The very principles for which the Allies were fighting, he argued in July 1918, must be used, as he put it, 'to protect the German people'. Once again, as at the time of the Boer War, he refused to be drawn into the anti-German hysteria of the day. Once German militarism was destroyed, the German people must be protected 'by those simple principles of right and freedom against which they will have warred so long in vain'.[2]

Believing that these principles of 'right and freedom' were at the centre both of Britain's own war exertions, and of the morality of Britain's war effort, Churchill argued in favour of a peace based on justice: no excessive reparations, no transfer of territory away from its ethnic inhabitants, no vindictive clauses. Asked, while in France, to devise an inscription for a war memorial, he wrote: 'In war, Resolution; in defeat, Defiance; in victory, Magnanimity; in peace, Goodwill.'[3] His inscription was not accepted. But it expressed his sentiments exactly.

At the time of the Paris Peace Conference, Churchill urged a generous peace with Germany, and opposed any threat to renew war if the Germans refused to sign the Treaty, telling the War Cabinet that he wished to see Germany 'treated humanely and adequately fed, and her industries restarted'.[4] As the Paris Peace Conference was coming to an end, he wrote to Lloyd George;

The newspapers and public opinion at home, so far as it is vocal, claims the enforcement of the most extreme terms upon the vanquished enemy. . . .

[1] Winston S. Churchill, *The World Crisis*, volume III, London, March 1927, page 339.
[2] Speech of 4 July 1918.
[3] Winston S. Churchill, *My Early Life*, London 1931, page 346.
[4] War Cabinet of 28 February 1919, quoted in *Churchill*, document volume 4, pages 556–8.

The same crowd that is now so vociferous for ruthless terms of peace will spin round to-morrow against the Government if a military breakdown occurs through the dwindling forces which are at our disposal. It is one thing to keep a compact force for a long time in comfortable billets around Cologne in a well administered and adequately rationed district. It is quite another to spread these young troops we have over large areas of Germany holding down starving populations, living in houses with famished women and children, and firing on miners and working people maddened by despair.

Disaster of the most terrible kind lies on that road, and I solemnly warn the Government of the peril of proceeding along it. A situation might soon be reached from which the British moral sentiment would recoil. I consider that we shall commit a political error of the first order if we are drawn into the heart of Germany in these conditions. We may easily be caught, as Napoleon was in Spain, and gripped in a position from which there is no retreat and where our strength will steadily be consumed . . .

In his letter Churchill went on to warn Lloyd George of the practical difficulties of trying 'to carve up and distribute at pleasure the populations of three or four enormous Empires with a few hundred thousand war-weary conscripts', and he declared:

Now is the time, and it may be the only time, to reap the fruits of victory. 'Agree with thine adversary whilst thou art in the way with him'. Everything shows that the present German Government is sincerely desirous of making a beaten peace and preserving an orderly community which will carry out its agreement. It seems to me quite natural that they should put forward a series of counter propositions, and we ought to take these up seriatim with patience and goodwill and endeavour to split the outstanding differences. In this way we shall get a genuine German acceptance of a defeated peace and not be drawn into new dangers measureless in their character.

The British Empire is in a very fine position at the present moment, and we now require a peace which will fix and recognise that position. Let us beware lest in following too far Latin ambitions and hatreds we do not create a new situation in which our advantages will largely have disappeared. Settle now while we have the power, or lose perhaps for ever the power of settlement on the basis of a military victory.[1]

[1] Letter of 20 May 1919, quoted in *Churchill*, document volume 4, pages 656-7.

Thirteen years later, this was still his theme. As he told the House of Commons, in opposing the Government's disarmament policy:

The removal of the just grievances of the vanquished ought to precede the disarmament of the victors. To bring about anything like equality of armaments if it were in our power to do so, which it happily is not, while those grievances remain unredressed, would be almost to appoint the day for another European war—to fix it as if it were a prize-fight. It would be far safer to reopen questions like those of the Dantzig Corridor and Transylvania, with all their delicacy and difficulty, in cold blood and in a calm atmosphere and while the victor nations still have ample superiority, than to wait and drift on, inch by inch and stage by stage, until once again vast combinations, equally matched confront each other face to face.[1]

It was not only a generous peace settlement, based on reconciliation, but also a continued national effort inside Britain, free from class conflicts, that Churchill had urged as a priority in the immediate aftermath of war, telling his constituents:

Why should war be the only purpose capable of uniting us in comradeship. Why should war be the only cause large enough to call forth really great and fine sacrifices? Look at the wonderful superb things people will do to carry on a war and to win a victory. Look what they will give up. Look what toils they achieve—what risks, what sufferings, what marvellous ingenuity, and what heroic and splendid qualities they display. All for war. Nothing is too good for war. Why cannot we have some of it for peace? Why is war to have all the splendours, all the nobleness, all the courage and loyalty? Why should peace have nothing but the squabbles and the selfishness and the pettiness of daily life? Why if men and women, all classes, all parties, are able to work together for five years like a mighty machine to produce *destruction*, can they not work together for another five years to produce *abundance*?

All the arts and science that we used in war are standing by us now ready to help us in peace. All the organised power which moved the fleets and armies, which hunted the submarines in the depths of the sea, which made us the victors in the air, which produced unlimited munitions of every intricate kind—all the clever brains, true brave

[1] House of Commons, 23 November 1932.

hearts, strong unwearied hands—all are available. Only one thing do we require—a common principle of action, a plain objective, that everyone can understand and work for, as he worked to beat the German. Without this we cannot succeed. But surely we have a common purpose? Surely this period of reconstruction may be looked upon as if it were a part of the war? Surely if the sense of self-preservation enabled us to combine to conquer the same sense of self-preservation should enable us to restore and revive our prosperity? . . .

In his peroration Churchill declared:

Five years of concerted effort by all classes, like what we have given in the war, but without its tragedies, would create an abundance and prosperity in this land, aye, throughout the world, such as has never yet been known or dreamt of. Five years of faction, of bickering, of class jealousies and Party froth, will not merely not give us prosperity, it will land us in utter and universal privation.

The Choice is in our own hands. Like the Israelites of old, blessing and cursing is set before us. To-day we can have the greatest failures or the greatest triumph—as we choose. There is enough for all. The earth is a generous mother. Never, never did science offer such fairy gifts to man. Never did their knowledge and organisation stand so high. Repair the waste. Rebuild the ruins. Heal the wounds. Crown the victors. Comfort the broken and broken-hearted. There is the battle we have now to fight. There is the victory we have now to win. Let us go forward together.[1]

*   *   *

Churchill's political philosophy was supremely simple in concept: it was based on the preservation and protection of individual freedom and a decent way of life, if necessary by means of State aid and power; on the protection of the individual against the misuse of State power; on the pursuit of political compromise and the middle way, in order both to maintain and to improve the existing framework of Parliamentary democracy; on the protection of small States against the aggression of more powerful States; and on the linking together of all democratic States to protect themselves from the curse and calamity of war.

[1] Speech of 26 November 1918, Gilbert, *Churchill*, volume 4, pages 171-2.

Though simple in concept, in execution this philosophy proved easy to abandon in most countries and by most leaders as the twentieth century progressed; and only when it was in fact too late to uphold these beliefs in the majority of the countries where they had once been welcomed, was Churchill called upon to attempt to save at least a part of them from the wreck.

III

WARNINGS AND REFLECTIONS
1925-1948

In the aftermath of the First World War, Churchill became increasingly concerned with the dangers of a renewal of European conflict, if wise policies were not followed. From his vantage point as a member of Lloyd George's peacetime Cabinet—first as Secretary of State for War and Air, and then as Secretary of State for the Colonies—he sought a foreign policy which would prevent what he saw as an otherwise inevitable renewal of what he called 'the European war'.

In the years immediately following the Paris Peace Conference, Churchill was a member of Lloyd George's Cabinet, first as Secretary of State for War and Air, and then as Secretary of State for the Colonies. Now with fifteen years' experience of Government, and twenty of Parliament, behind him, he spoke with a conviction born both of experience and disappointment. His fear was the collapse of democratic Government throughout Europe: 'Russia has gone into ruin . . .' he wrote to Lloyd George in March 1920. 'But Germany may perhaps still be saved.' And he went on to explain:

You ought to tell France that we will make a defensive alliance with her against Germany if *and only if* she entirely alters her treatment of Germany & loyally accepts a British policy of help & friendship towards Germany. Next you shd send a great man to Berlin to help consolidate the anti-Sparticist anti-Ludendorff elements into a strong left centre block. For this task you have two levers 1. Food & credit, wh must be generously accorded in spite of our own difficulties (wh otherwise will worsen) 2ndly Early revision of the Peace Treaty by a Conference to wh New Germany shall be invited as an equal partner in the rebuilding of Europe. Using these levers it ought to be possible to rally all that is good & stable in the German nation . . .[1]

Churchill understood the French predicament, which he set out in a draft memorandum for his Cabinet colleagues in August 1920. 'France is unreasonable', he wrote, 'because she is terrified. She sees forces massing up against her in the East. She sees herself abandoned by the United States. She is convinced Britain means to detach herself.' Churchill's answer was a 'binding alliance' between Britain, France, and Germany. In return for German friendship, France would obtain the security she desired against any other potential enemy. But to win German friendship, Churchill stressed, 'implies a profound revision of the Treaty of Versailles, and the acceptance of Germany as an equal partner in the future guidance of Europe . . .'.[2]

A year later, at the Imperial Conference in London, Churchill explained his view of what should be done in Europe to the Prime Ministers of Australia, Canada, and New Zealand:

The aim is to get an appeasement of the fearful hatreds and antagonisms which exist in Europe and to enable the world to settle down. I have no other object in view.

I feel that a greater assurance to France would be a foundation for that. First of all, our duty towards France in this matter is rather an obvious one because she gave up her claims—very illegitimate claims as we thought them, but she waived them—to take a strong strategic position along the Rhine which her Marshals advised her to do, and this Anglo-American guarantee was intended to be a substitute to France. We said to her, if you give up the strategical position, England and America will be with you in the hour of need. Well, America did not make good, and one would have thought France all the more would have needed the British Empire, but it is a fact that the Treaty is naturally invalidated by America not having made good and France got neither Britain nor America, nor did she get her strategic frontier on the Rhine. The result of that is undoubtedly to have created a deep fear in the heart of France, and a fear which anyone can understand

---

[1] Letter of 24 March 1920, *Churchill*, document volume 4, pages 1053-5.
[2] Draft memorandum, 29 August 1920, *Churchill*, document volume 4, pages 1190-4.

who looks at the population of the two countries, one declining and already under forty millions—38 millions—and the other bounding up, in spite of all that has happened, with great masses of military youths reaching manhood, and in seven or eight years replacing the losses of the war.

No one can doubt the deep rooted nature of the fear which this poor mutilated, impoverished France has of this mighty Germany which is growing up on the other side of the Rhine. It is this fear, if I may say so with all respect to the Conference which is the explanation and to a certain extent the excuse for the intolerant and violent action which France is taking. If at any time the means arises of reducing that fear, of giving such an assurance, I think we ought to consider it very carefully indeed.

Churchill wanted the Imperial Prime Ministers to look sympathetically at French fears. But he also wanted a positive policy of reconciliation towards Germany, and this too he explained to them:

I am anxious to see friendship grow up and the hatred of the war die between Britain and Germany. I am anxious to see trade relations develop with Germany naturally and harmoniously. I am anxious to see Britain getting all the help and use she can out of Germany in the difficult years that lie before us.

I am very much afraid that any friendly relations which grow up in time between Britain and Germany will be terribly suspect to France. France will say 'You are changing sides; you are going over to the other side. We are to be left to ourselves, and England is more the friend of Germany than of France.'

But I think if a Treaty were in existence which in the ultimate issue, in the extreme issue, bound the British Empire to protect France, against unprovoked aggression, we could always point to that and say, 'No, if you are attacked, there is our scrap of paper; we shall be as good as our word next time as we were last time.' That will give you greater freedom, in my humble opinion, to establish new relations, new co-operation with Germany in the further reconstruction and rebuilding of Europe, and it might well be that being at once the Ally of France and the friend of Germany, we might be in a position to mitigate the frightful rancour and fear and hatred which exist between France and Germany at the present time and which, if left unchecked, will most certainly in a generation or so bring about a renewal of the struggle of which we have just witnessed the conclusion.[1]

Churchill's philosophy of appeasement—what he was later to call 'appeasement from strength'—found little favour. The anti-Germanism of the immediate post-war world was strong. But believing as he did that the peace could only be preserved in Europe if the victors embarked as soon as possible upon practical measures of conciliation, he reiterated this advice at the beginning of 1925 when, as Chancellor of the Exchequer, he called on President Doumergue in Paris, telling the President:

... of course I was only expressing a personal opinion, but one which I had expressed in public on many occasions, and which it was well known I had held for several years, namely, that the one real security against a renewal of war would be a complete agreement between England, France and Germany. That alone would give the security which all were seeking, and that alone would enable the commerce of Europe to expand to such dimensions that the existing burden of debts and reparations would be supportable and not crushing.

Churchill added that it would be better to come to good terms with Germany, and to settle her grievances, than to have a defensive alliance between France and Britain 'while the fundamental antagonism between France and Germany continued unappeased'.[2]

Returning to Britain, Churchill urged his new Conservative colleagues to bring Germany into any western European security pact, and to revise the Versailles Treaty as far as Germany's eastern frontier with Poland was concerned. It was for Britain, he urged, to take the initiative to bring about 'a real peace' between France and Germany, first satisfying Germany's post-Versailles grievances, and then offering security guarantees simultaneously to Germany and France.[3]

Churchill's idea was opposed by Austen Chamberlain, the Foreign Secretary, by Sir Maurice Hankey, and by A. J. Balfour. The Locarno Pact, when it came, made no provision for frontier

[1] Imperial Conference minutes, 7 July 1921, quoted in Gilbert, *Churchill*, volume 4, pages 607-9.

[2] Account of a conversation (sent to Austen Chamberlain, the Foreign Secretary), 11 January 1925, *Churchill*, document volume 5, 'The Exchequer Years', pages 338-40.

[3] Committee of Imperial Defence, 13 February 1925, quoted in Gilbert, *Churchill*, volume 5, pages 122-4.

changes. The German grievance remained. And as Churchill had warned both in London and Paris, if that grievance was left unappeased while Britain and France were strong, revision would eventually be brought about by war, once the balance of power had swung in Germany's favour. This was his overriding fear throughout the twelve years between the signature of the Versailles Treaty and Hitler's coming to power.

Churchill's emphasis on the tripartite link between Britain, France, and Germany, and on the need for an immediate and substantial revision of the Versailles Treaty, arose from two related feelings: the fear of a revived and vengeful Germany on the one hand, and, on the other, the weakness of the western European democracies in face of the Soviet challenge. For this reason he had urged Lloyd George, in 1920, to strengthen the democratic forces in Weimar Germany. Indeed, as early as November 1918, on the day *before* the armistice, he had told the War Cabinet: 'We might have to build up the German Army, as it was important to get Germany on her legs again, for fear of the spread of Bolshevism.'[1]

In Churchill's mind, Bolshevism was an evil system, totally destructive of all the freedoms, and all the human values, in which he believed. An enemy of tyranny for more than twenty years, it was the supreme tyranny, crushing all of the liberties he prized. Even in its early days, when Bolshevik sailors had shot down Captain Cromie, the British Naval Attaché, inside the Petrograd Embassy, he had been outraged, telling the War Cabinet: 'The exertions which a nation is prepared to make to protect its individual representatives or citizens from outrage is one of the truest measures of its greatness as an organised State.'[2]

Every subsequent piece of information which reached him confirmed him in the view that Bolshevism was totally destructive of individual liberty. At first he hoped that it would, as he told his colleagues, 'be exposed and swept away by a General Election', held if necessary under 'Allied auspices'.[3] Later he

[1] War Cabinet, 10 November 1918, quoted in *Churchill*, document volume 4, page 412.

[2] War Cabinet paper (draft), 4 September 1918, quoted in Gilbert, *Churchill*, volume 4, page 225.

[3] Imperial War Cabinet, minutes, 31 December 1918, quoted in Gilbert, *Churchill*, volume 4, pages 228–30.

sought to strengthen the existing Allied support for each of the anti-Bolshevik Russian armies pressing in at different times upon Moscow and Petrograd. But his main task, imposed upon him by Lloyd George, and carried out with reluctance, was actually to withdraw the British troops which Lloyd George himself had sent a year earlier to help the Russian anti-Bolsheviks.

Yet Churchill was convinced that unless Bolshevism were overthrown, Western democracy and civilization would be threatened, and might even be destroyed. As he wrote of Lenin, Trotsky, and the other Bolshevik leaders:

Theirs is a war against civilised society which can never end. They seek as the first condition of their being the overthrow and destruction of all existing institutions and of every State and Government now standing in the world. They too aim at a worldwide and international league, but a league of the failures, the criminals, the unfit, the mutinous, the morbid, the deranged, and the distraught in every land; and between them and such order of civilisation as we have been able to build up since the dawn of history there can, as Lenin rightly proclaims, be neither truce nor pact.[1]

Churchill feared, above all, a Bolshevik and militaristic Russia which, in alliance with a Germany whose post-Versailles grievances had not been met, would undermine all the achievements of victory and peacemaking. In November 1919 he tried to explain his position to the French Minister of Munitions, Louis Loucheur:

Understand, my friend, that I am not thinking of any immediate danger, but only of the dangers of five or ten years hence. I fear more than I can express the re-union of Russia and Germany, both determined to get back what they have lost in the war, the one through being our ally, the other through being our foe, and both convinced that acting together they will be irresistible. . . .

I am young enough to have to look ahead so far as the future of my own country is concerned, and I am bound to say, speaking of the years which lie before us, that I should deeply regret to see England involved in such a hopeless situation.[2]

[1] *Weekly Dispatch*, 22 June 1919.
[2] Letter of 21 November 1919, Loucheur papers, quoted in *Churchill*, document volume 4, pages 963-5.

It was the tyrannical aspect of Lenin's regime that most roused his fury. Writing in January 1920 he declared:

A Tyrant is one who allows the fancies of his mind to count for more in deciding action than the needs, feeling, hopes, lives and physical well-being of the people over whom he has obtained control. A tyrant is one who wrecks the lives of millions for the satisfaction of his own conceptions. So far as possible in this world no man should have such power, whether under an imperialist, republican, militarist, socialist or soviet form of Government. . . .[1]

In May 1920 Churchill set out his view of Bolshevik tyranny in a Cabinet memorandum. The Bolsheviks, he wrote, have 'committed, and are committing unspeakable atrocities, and are maintaining themselves in power by a terrorism on an unprecedented scale, and by the denial of the most elementary rights of citizenship of freedom'.[2]

Churchill's hatred of Bolshevism, sprang from his belief that the ultimate aim of the Communist philosophy was the complete destruction of Parliamentary democracy, personal liberty, and free speech. He had, of course, followed the events of the post-revolutionary Russia closely: the suppression by Lenin of the Constituent Assembly—with its already predominantly proletarian franchise—Trotsky's brutal suppression of the Kronstadt revolt, the closing of churches, and the killing of priests. He had no need to await the publication of Solzhenitzyn's 'gulag' to know the fate of the hundreds of thousands of political prisoners of the 1920s. And to an audience at Sunderland he set out the points of difference as he saw them:

We believe in Parliamentary Government exercised in accordance with the will of the majority of the electors constitutionally and freely ascertained. They seek to overthrow Parliament by direct action or other violent means . . . and then to rule the mass of the nation in accordance with their theories, which have never yet been applied successfully, and through the agency of self-elected or sham-elected caucuses of their own.

[1] *Illustrated Sunday Herald*, 25 January 1920.
[2] Cabinet memorandum, 1 May 1920, copy, Edward Marsh papers, quoted in *Churchill*, document volume 4, pages 1077–8.

They seek to destroy capital. We seek to control monopolies. They seek to eradicate the idea of individual possession. We seek to use the great mainspring of human endeavour as a means of increasing the volume of production on every side and of sharing the fruits far more broadly and evenly among millions of individual homes. We defend freedom of conscience and religious equality. They seek to exterminate every form of religious belief that has given comfort and inspiration to the soul of man. . . .[1]

In August 1920 the Red Army advanced into Poland, approaching within a few miles of Warsaw. Even Lloyd George was so horrified that he delivered—six years to the day after Britain's declaration of war on Germany—an ultimatum to the Bolsheviks to halt their forces. In the event, it was a Polish victory, the so-called 'Miracle of the Vistula', not the British ultimatum, which saved Polish independence. At the moment when the Red Army seemed poised for victory, Churchill had written an article in the *Evening News*:

It is easy for those who live a long way from the Russian Bolshevists,—especially those who are protected by a good strip of salt water, and who stand on the firm rock of an active political democracy—to adopt a cool and airy view of their Communist doctrines and machinations.

But a new, weak, impoverished, famishing State like Poland, itself quaking internally, is placed in hourly jeopardy by close and continuous contact with such neighbours.

The Bolshevik aim of world revolution can be pursued equally in peace or war. In fact, a Bolshevist peace is only another form of war.

If they do not for the moment overwhelm with armies, they can undermine with propaganda.

Not a shot may be fired along the whole front, not a bayonet may be fixed, not a battalion may move, and yet invasion may be proceeding swiftly and relentlessly. The peasants are roused against the landlords, the workmen against their employers, the railways and public services are induced to strike, the soldiers are incited to mutiny and kill their officers, the mob are raised against the middle classes to murder them, to plunder their houses, to steal their belongings, to debauch their

---

[1] Speech of 1 January 1920. It was at this meeting that Anthony Eden heard Churchill speak for the first time. The speech is quoted in Gilbert, *Churchill*, volume 4, pages 365-6.

wives and carry off their children; an elaborate network of secret societies entangles honest political action; the Press is bought wherever possible.

This was what Poland dreaded and will now have reason to dread still more; and this was the cause, even more than the gathering of the Russian armies on the Polish front, continuous for nearly a year, that led the Poles to make that desperate military sally or counter-stroke which English Liberal opinion has so largely misunderstood, and which Socialist opinion has so successfully misrepresented.

Assuming that Poland was about to be overrun altogether, Churchill ended his article with an appeal to the Germans to take this opportunity of winning the gratitude and support of the victors:

It will be open to the Germans either to sink their own social structure in the general Bolshevist welter and spread the reign of chaos far and wide throughout the Continent; or, on the other hand, by a supreme effort of sobriety, of firmness, of self-restraint and of courage—undertaken, as most great exploits have to be, under conditions of peculiar difficulty and discouragement—to build a dyke of peaceful, lawful, patient strength and virtue against the flood of red barbarism flowing from the East, and thus safeguard their own interests and the interests of their principal antagonists in the West.[1]

Churchill's detestation of Communism was complete. Yet the centre of his political philosophy was the survival of parliamentary democracy. And to ensure this survival, he was prepared to consider any expedient. Twice in his lifetime this included the expedient of working with Communist Russia as an active ally. The first occasion was in the summer of 1918, after the German breakthrough on the Western Front: a breakthrough only made possible because the Russia of Lenin and Trotsky had made its peace with Germany, thus liberating millions of men for active service in the Western Front. To halt the German advance, Churchill proposed a deal with the Bolsheviks: if they would reopen the Eastern Front against Germany, then Britain (and America) would guarantee the permanence of the Bolshevik revolution. 'Let us never forget', he

[1] *Evening News*, 28 July 1920.

told the Cabinet, 'that Lenin and Trotsky are fighting with ropes round their necks. Show them any real chance of consolidating their power, of getting some kind of protection against the vengeance of a counter-revolution, and they would be non-human not to embrace it.'[1]

Twenty years later, when Hitler's dominance of Europe was almost complete, Churchill again argued in favour of an alliance with the Soviet Union. Even when Stalin turned, instead, to Hitler, and seized the eastern third of Poland, Churchill never abandoned his belief that Russia would eventually be brought in as an ally. When, in June 1941, Hitler attacked the Soviet Union, Churchill immediately offered Russia all the military and economic assistance which Britain could provide (and did provide, at considerable cost), telling the British people:

The Nazi régime is indistinguishable from the worst features of Communism. It is devoid of all theme and principle except appetite and racial domination. It excels all forms of human wickedness in the efficiency of its cruelty and ferocious aggression. No one has been a more consistent opponent of Communism than I have for the last twenty-five years. I will unsay no word that I have spoken about it. But all this fades away before the spectacle which is now unfolding. The past with its crimes, its follies and its tragedies, flashes away. . . .

We have but one aim and one single, irrevocable purpose. We are resolved to destroy Hitler and every vestige of the Nazi régime. From this nothing will turn us—nothing.

That is our policy and that is our declaration. It follows, therefore, that we shall give whatever help we can to Russia and to the Russian people. We shall appeal to all our friends and allies in every part of the world to take the same course and pursue it, as we shall, faithfully and steadfastly to the end.

Churchill went on to explain that Britain had already offered the Soviet Union 'any technical or economic assistance which is in our power, and which is likely to be of service to them'.[2]

The summers of 1918 and 1940 were extreme cases of British

---

[1] Draft memorandum of 7 April 1918, printed in full in *Churchill*, document volume 5, 'The Coming of War'.

[2] Broadcast of 22 June 1941, quoted in Winston S. Churchill, *War Speeches*, volume 2, pages 176-80.

danger. Hence Churchill's willingness to contemplate, and indeed to urge, a direct Anglo-Soviet alliance. But it was not only in times of danger that he was in favour of compromise in Anglo-Soviet relations. War for the sake of war had no part in his philosophy, nor did he see any virtue in supporting a cause that was lost. In the interests of preserving what could be preserved of European democracy, he was eager to bring about a compromise. As he wrote to the leader of one of the anti-Bolshevik Russian armies, General Denikin, whose forces had been driven back from central Russia to the southern Ukraine:

Great changes are taking place in the character and organisation of the Bolshevik Government. In spite of the hellish wickedness in which it was founded and has been developed, it nevertheless represents a force of order: the men at the head are no longer merely revolutionaries but persons who having seized power are anxious to retain it and enjoy it for a time. They are believed earnestly to desire peace, fearing no doubt if war continues to be devoured later on by their own armies. A period of peace coupled with commercial reorganisation may well prepare the way for the unity of Russia through a political evolution.[1]

General Denikin rejected all ideas of negotiating with the Bolsheviks, or, as Churchill urged, of declaring independence in the small regions under his control, and then negotiating with the Bolsheviks. Within two months General Denikin had been replaced by General Wrangel, and the anti-Bolshevik Russians had been driven further back, into the Crimea. Once again, Churchill urged the opening of negotiations with the Bolsheviks, and the search for a compromise peace. This time he proposed a British initiative, writing to Lloyd George:

I shd be prepared to make peace with Soviet Russia on the best terms available to appease the general situation, while safe-guarding us from being poisoned by them. I do not of course believe that any real harmony is possible between Bolshevism & present civilisation. But in view of the existing facts a cessation of arms & a promotion of material prosperity are inevitable: & we must trust for better or for worse to peaceful influences to bring about the disappearance of this awful tyranny & peril. . . .[2]

---

[1] Letter of 3 February 1920, quoted in *Churchill*, document volume 4, pages 1026-8.
[2] Letter of 24 March 1920, quoted in *Churchill*, document volume 4, pages 1053-5.

As the situation worsened for General Wrangel, Churchill put more detailed proposals before a conference of ministers whom Lloyd George had authorized to begin negotiations with Soviet Russia for a trade treaty. Churchill had a more ambitious scheme, telling his colleagues:

. . . that the British Government should offer to the Soviet Government their whole-hearted co-operation in concerting a Peace between the Soviet Government, on the one hand, and General Wrangel and the Polish Government on the other. The agreement in regard to General Wrangel should provide that the Crimea should form an Asylum for the remnants of the classes opposed to the Bolsheviks, and that immunity from Bolshevist advances should be granted to the Crimea for at least a year. If such an arrangement was come to it was thought that the situation in Russia would be greatly improved and would permit of the Russian refugees now in the Crimea returning under amnesty to Russia.

In return, the British Government should insist on a comprehensive agreement which should cover the various points at issue between the Soviet Government and this country, namely, the return of prisoners from Russia, and Bolshevist interference in Afghanistan, Persia and the Caucasus. The agreement should also cover Bolshevist propaganda in the United Kingdom, Allied countries and Central Europe. . . .[1]

Churchill's advocacy of a negotiated peace with the Bolsheviks in no way lessened his detestation of their political system. But one constant factor of his political philosophy was a continual attempt—no month of his life passed without it—to assess the realities of the European situation, the lines of likely change, and the extent to which these changes would constitute a threat to those areas of the democratic world—what later became known as the Free World—over which Britain had the power or influence to be effective. In this assessment, he tried to foresee in realistic terms what would come to pass, before then seeking solutions—if such there were—for what was to be done. As he wrote at the height of the Russo-Polish war in 1920:

Possibly in two stages, under some camouflage or other, the Russian part of Poland will be re-absorbed in the Russian system. I apprehend

[1] Conference of Ministers, minutes, 28 May 1920, quoted in Gilbert, *Churchill*, volume 4, pages 398–400.

the same fate will speedily overtake Lithuania, Latvia and Esthonia. These Baltic Provinces of Russia, the conquests of Peter the Great, will never be suffered to remain outside Russian Bolshevik control. As for Finland, partly by revolution from within, partly by attack from without, her turn will come.

But, after all, the reincorporation within the limits of the Russian Empire of these former Russian States that had not the wit to defend themselves in common, though a melancholy event, is not in itself a decisive event in European history. I have always believed that Russia would regain her 1914 frontiers and would never rest till she had done so. I had hoped, however, that she would have regained them under a Government friendly to the Allies, loyal to them in the War, and hostile to Germany. The disastrous fact for France, & also for us, is that they will be regained by a Russian Government fundamentally hostile to France and, indeed, to all the Allies. . . .[1]

It was to avoid the linking-up of Germany with the Bolshevik system, as a result of what he called 'a combination of interest and of policy', that Churchill went on to propose the immediate revision of the Versailles Treaty, followed by the linking of a satisfied and *un*vengeful Weimar Germany in a defensive alliance with Britain and France.

*   *   *

Here then were the three interwoven strands of Churchill's political philosophy: 'the appeasement of class bitterness' at home, 'the appeasement of the fearful hatreds and antagonisms abroad', and the defence of Parliamentary democracy and democratic values in Britain, in Western Europe, and in the territories under British rule or control. Wherever possible, the method to be used was conciliation, the route to be chosen was the middle way, the path of moderation. But where force alone could preserve the libertarian values, force would have to be used. It could only be a last resort—the horrors of war, and the very nature of democracy, ensured that—but in the last resort it might be necessary to defend those values by force of arms.

By 1921 these three strands, and all their ramifications, were clear in Churchill's mind. He was forty-four years old (my age

[1] Draft memorandum, 29 August 1920, quoted in *Churchill*, document volume 4, pages 1190–4.

today!), and he could look back on twenty years of public life, including four wartime years, through almost all of which he had been an active participant at the centre of policymaking, arguing his points with men of experience and expertise, testing his ideas amid the daily pressure of departmental business, and reflecting, with each year, on the evolution of the world scene, and the nature of man.

These reflection were sometimes sombre. As Churchill told his constituents on 11 November 1922, six years after the armistice:

> What a disappointment the Twentieth Century has been
> How terrible & how melancholy
>   is long series of disastrous events
>   wh have darkened its first 20 years.
> We have seen in ev country a dissolution,
>   a weakening of those bonds,
>   a challenge to those principles
>   a decay of faith
>   an abridgement of hope
>   on wh structure & ultimate existence
>   of civilized society depends.
> We have seen in ev part of globe
>   one gt country after another
>   wh had erected an orderly, a peaceful
>   a prosperous structure of civilised society,
>   relapsing in hideous succession
>   into bankruptcy, barbarism or anarchy.

Churchill then spoke of each of the areas which were in turmoil: China and Mexico 'sunk into confusion'; Russia, where 'that little set of Communist criminals ... have exhausted millions of the Russian people'; Ireland scene of an 'enormous retrogression of civilisation & Christianity'; Egypt and India, where 'we see among millions of people hitherto shielded by superior science & superior law a desire to shatter the structure by which they live & to return blindly & heedlessly to primordial chaos'. He then went on to warn of the future:

> Can you doubt, my faithful friends
>   as you survey this sombre panorama,

that mankind is passing through a period marked
  not only by an enormous destruction
  & abridgement of human species,
    not only by a vast impoverishment
    & reduction in means of existence
  but also that destructive tendencies
    have not yet run their course?
And only intense, concerted & prolonged efforts
  among all nations
    can avert further & perhaps even greater calamities.[1]

Henceforth, during his remaining forty years of public life Churchill's actions were to be in harmony with his philosophy. Henceforth, he was to apply to new events, new problems, new upheavals, the lessons and conclusions of his first twenty years in public life. Immediately, in 1921 and 1922, he was to take the lead, at Lloyd George's instigation and to the distress of many Conservatives, in seeking a compromise solution in Ireland — the defence and practical evolution of the Irish Treaty of 1922.

The Irish debates of 1922 marked also a high point of Churchill's Parliamentary skills, and a confirmation of his mastery of the art of presentation of a complex and controversial subject, at a time of crisis, to a cynical House of Commons. Here, too, his was the voice of sympathy and reconciliation, following four years of civil war and bitterness.[2]

Even while the Irish negotiations proceeded, Churchill, as Secretary of State for the Colonies, sought to satisfy Zionist aspirations by supporting a series of practical measures for the building up of a Jewish National Home in Palestine, while at the same time seeking to satisfy Arab aspirations by the installation of Arab rulers in Iraq and Transjordan, and the safeguarding of Arab rights in Palestine. Although overruled by the Middle East experts, he also argued in favour of Kurdish autonomy in the upper Euphrates, fearing an Iraqi ruler who would, as he put it, 'ignore Kurdish sentiment and oppress the Kurdish minoritys'.[3]

---

[1] Quoted in Gilbert, *Churchill*, volume 4, page 915.

[2] For Churchill's part in the working out of the Irish settlement, see Gilbert, *Churchill*, volume 4, chapters 26, 37, 38, 39 and 40.

[3] Cairo Conference, transcript, 15 March 1921, quoted in Gilbert, *Churchill*, volume 4, pages 544-7.

In India, he had upheld, before a hostile House of Commons, the censure of General Dyer for opening fire on an Indian mob that was unarmed. 'Frightfulness', Churchill told those Conservative MPs who wanted the General reinstated — 'Frightfulness is not a remedy known to the British pharmacopoeia.'

Pressed continually to support the use of force in India, as used by General Dyer, Churchill set out for the House of Commons his philosophy of imperial rule: a philosophy formed fifteen years before, when he had been Under-Secretary of State in the same Government department:

> . . . as we contemplate the great physical forces and the power at the disposal of the British Government in their relations with the native population of India, we ought to remember the words of Macaulay— *'and then was seen what we believe to be the most frightful of all spectacles, the strength of civilisation without its mercy.'*
>
> Our reign in India or anywhere else has never stood on the basis of physical force alone, and it would be fatal to the British Empire if we were to try to base ourselves only upon it. The British way of doing things has always meant and implied close and effectual co-operation with the people of the country. In every part of the British Empire that has been our aim, and in no part have we arrived at such success as in India, whose princes spent their treasure in our cause, whose brave soldiers fought side by side with our own men, whose intelligent and gifted people are co-operating at the present moment with us in every sphere of government and of industry.[1]

These feelings about India were sincere. Churchill was a supporter of the Montagu–Chelmsford reforms of 1919, and of the Simon report a decade later. But when he saw what he regarded as the triumph of extremism over moderation in India, he resisted the transfer of effective power from the Raj to the Congress. Churchill, and the India Defence League MPs who gathered around him, feared a growing Hindu dominance, not only over the despised Muslim minority, but over the hated untouchables.

Churchill also feared that the loosening of the bonds and morality of Empire would lead to a weakening of Britain's faith in itself, at a time when European tyrannies were challenging

[1] House of Commons, 8 July 1920.

the whole will and fibre of democratic life. For Churchill, the will to rule, and the beneficient fibre of the British colonial and imperial structure of the 1930s were two facets of a single theme: the underlying quality of democracry, and its universal strength and application. As Churchill wrote to his close friend Lord Linlithgow, one of the leading advocates of the new India Bill:

I think we differ principally in this, that you assume the future is a mere extension of the past whereas I find history full of unexpected turns and retrogressions. The mild and vague Liberalism of the early years of the twentieth century, the surge of fantastic hopes and illusions that followed the armistice of the Great War have already been superseded by a violent reaction against Parliamentary and election-eering procedure and by the establishment of dictatorships real or veiled in almost every country. Moreover the loss of our external connections, the shrinkage in foreign trade and shipping brings the surplus population of Britain within measurable distance of utter ruin. We are entering a period when the struggle for self-preservation is going to present itself with great intenseness to thickly populated industrial countries.

It is unsound reasoning therefore to suppose that England alone among the nations will be willing to part with her control over a great dependency like India. The Dutch will not do it; the French will not do it; the Italians will not do it. As for the Japanese, they are conquering a new empire. All the time you and your friends go on mouthing the bland platitudes of an easy safe triumphant age which has passed away, whereas, the tide has turned and you will be engulfed by it.

In my view England is now beginning a new period of struggle and fighting for its life, and the crux of it will be not only the retention of India but a much stronger assertion of commercial rights. As long as we are sure that we press no claim on India which is not in their real interest we are justified in using our undoubted power for their welfare and for our own.[1]

Yet when Churchill's India campaign had failed and the India Defence League was disbanded, he told the new Viceroy, who was to operate the pact, 'you need not expect anything but silence or help from us',[2] and he told his constituents:

[1] Quoted in Gilbert *Churchill*, volume 5, pages 480–1.
[2] Letter of 8 August 1935, quoted in Gilbert, *Churchill*, volume 5, page 617.

I am reminded of the words which the late Lord Salisbury, then Lord Cranborne, used after the fierce and bitter controversy about the Reform Bill of 1867. He said—'It is the duty of every Englishman, and of every English party to accept a political defeat cordially, and to lend their best endeavours to secure the success, or to neutralise the evil, of the principles to which they have been forced to succumb.[1]

As a gesture of conciliation, Churchill invited one of Gandhi's leading supporters, G. D. Birla, to lunch at Chartwell. Their meeting was amicable: indeed, as Birla wrote to Gandhi, it was 'one of my most pleasant experiences'. Churchill told Birla: 'Mr Gandhi has gone very high in my esteem since he stood up for the untouchables', and he went on, according to Birla's own record of the conversation:

'Well you have the opportunity now. I do not like the Bill but it is now on the Statute Book. I am not going to bother any more, but do not give us a chance to say that we anticipated a breakdown. The diehards would be pleased if there was a breakdown. You have got immense powers. Theoretically the Governors have all the powers, but in practice they have none. The King has all the powers in theory but none in practice. Socialists here had all the powers when they come into office, but they did not do anything radical. The Governors will never use the safeguards. So make it a success.'

I said, 'What is your test of success?' He said, 'My test is improvement in the lot of the masses, morally as well as materially. I do not care whether you are more or less loyal to Great Britain.'

Churchill's final words to Birla were:

I am genuinely sympathetic towards India. I have got real fears about the future. India, I feel is a burden on us. We have to maintain an army and for the sake of India we have to maintain Singapore and Near East strength. If India could look after herself we would be delighted. After all, the span of life is very small and I would not be too selfish. I would be only too delighted if the Reforms are a success. I have all along felt that there are fifty Indias. But you have got the things now; make it a success and if you do I will advocate your getting much more.[2]

*   *   *

[1] Letter of 25 August 1935, quoted in Gilbert, *Churchill*, volume 5, page 617.

[2] Record in Birla papers, quoted in full in *Churchill*, document volume 5, 'The Wilderness Years'.

Churchill still believed that India, even with the enormous measures of self-government of the 1935 Act, would remain, as the Act itself intended, as Ramsay MacDonald and as Baldwin intended, within the British Empire. Later, a phrase of his was to be much quoted: 'I have not become the King's first Minister in order to preside over the liquidation of the British Empire.'

Churchill had gone on to say, in his next sentence—a sentence which I have never seen quoted: 'For that task, if ever it were prescribed, someone else would have to be found, and, under democracy, I suppose the nation would have to be consulted.'[1] When within six years, a new Government did pursue a different course, Churchill accepted the decision of the majority, and did it, not sulkily, but emphatically, telling the House of Commons, as India and Pakistan became independent States:

Our Imperial mission in India is at at end—we must recognise that. Some day justice will be done by world opinion to our record there, but the chapter is closed. . . .

We must look forward. It is our duty, whatever part we have taken in the past, to hope and pray for the well-being and happiness of all the peoples of India, of whatever race, religion, social condition or historic character they may be. We must wish them all well and do what we can to help them on their road. Sorrow may lie in our hearts but bitterness and malice must be purged from them, and in our future more remote relations with India we must rise above all prejudice and partiality—and not allow our vision to be clouded by memories of glories that are gone for ever. And in this temper we shall find true guidance—and, indeed, our only hope—in strict and faithful adherence to the underlying principles of justice and freedom which are embodied in the United Nations organisation, and for the maintenance of which that instrument of world government was consciously created.

It is those principles, and those principles alone, which must govern our attitude and action towards this vast branch of toiling and suffering humanity. We have long had no interest in India which counted for more with us than the well-being and peace of its peoples. So far as we may be involved in the fortunes of the Indian peoples, and of the Governments of Pakistan and Hindustan, we must judge them,

[1] Speech of 10 November 1942, Mansion House, London, quoted in Winston S. Churchill, *The End of the Beginning* (war speeches), London 1943, pages 213-16.

not by race or religion, but impartially, by their future conduct to one another in accordance with the principles of the United Nations organisation under the Charter of human liberties which is being drawn up, and we must use our influence, such as it may be, against aggression, oppression and tyranny, from whatever quarter it comes. These principles alone must rule our actions, must enable us to steer our course in the incalculable tides on which we and our Indian fellow subjects are now embarked.[1]

*   *   *

Following the defeat of the Conservatives at the General Election of 1929, Churchill had spoken of retirement. He was already fifty-four years old, a senior Privy Councillor, and an elder statesman. His dream of 1924, that the 5 million Liberal voters would find a new and acceptable home within the Conservative Party was even more remote in 1929. L. S. Amery recorded Churchill's words to him that autumn: 'He had been all he ever wanted to be, short of the highest post, which he saw no prospect of . . .'[2]

If the liberal Toryism for which Churchill had argued in 1924, and for which he had planned while Chancellor of the Exchequer between 1925 and 1929, were not to come to pass; if, as he wrote, Neville Chamberlain or 'someone of that sort' were to lead the Tory Party, 'I clear out of politics'.[3]

Churchill's belief in Parliamentary democracy was such, however, that when he saw it endangered, he returned to politics: first to assert the supremacy of Parliament in making the decisions on the future of India, and then to insist that Parliament must turn its support to direct the policy of rearmament, the Covenant of the League of Nations, and alliances with other democratic states confronted by the growing threat of totalitarianism, as embodied in Nazi Germany.

As early as the unsuccessful Hitler–Ludendorff putsch in Munich in 1924, Churchill had told his constituents: 'we have no need now to seek our inspiration from Moscow or from Munich'.[4]

[1] House of Commons, 28 October 1948.

[2] L. S. Amery, diary, 5 August 1929, quoted in Gilbert, *Churchill*, volume 5, page 339.

[3] Letter to his wife, 27 August 1929, quoted in *Churchill*, document volume 5, 'The Wilderness Years'.

[4] Election Manifesto, 12 October 1924, quoted in *Churchill*, document volume 5, 'The Exchequer Years'.

And to the Italian Facists he said, at the height of his period of support for Mussolini's anti-communist policies: 'We have our own way of dong things.'[1]

For Churchill, that 'way' did not include submission to the dictates of force. As he wrote to Baldwin in 1927, after the Cabinet had decided to send troops to Hankow, where British lives and property were being threatened by local warlords and several British traders had been murdered:

> Short of being actually conquered, there is no evil worse than submitting to wrong and violence for fear of war. Once you take the position of not being able in any circumstances to defend your rights against the aggression of some particular set of people, there is no end to the demands that will be made or to the humiliations that must be accepted.[2]

Such was a central theme of Churchill's political philosophy in regard to defence and foreign affairs. Expressed so clearly in 1927, it was to guide him steadily through the period of Nazi aggrandizement that was soon to emerge. Combined with his hatred of tyranny, it was to mould and shape his reaction to Nazism, from Nazism's earliest days, even before Hitler came to power. Indeed, in October 1930, as reports of Nazi violence and racism had begun to feature in the British press, Churchill met a leading German diplomat at the German Embassy in London. The diplomat noted in a secret memorandum that Churchill had been following newspaper reports of events in Germany 'in detail', that he was 'pleased about the parliamentary victory of the Brüning government', but that he expressed himself 'in cutting terms' on National Socialism.

It was the Nazis, Churchill said, who had 'contributed towards a considerable deterioration of Germany's external position', particularly towards France, and he went on to tell the diplomat that 'France was still afraid of Germany', as she had been five years before, and that it was 'no bad thing for Europe' that France had a strong army, as the French 'were not an

---

[1] Press interview, 21 January 1927, quoted in Gilbert, *Churchill*, volume 5, pages 225–6.

[2] Letter of 22 January 1927, quoted in *Churchill*, document volume 5, 'The Exchequer Years'.

aggressive people and would never think if making an unprovoked attack on Germany'. The Maginot Line which the
French were building was the 'tangible' expression of French
fears. The diplomat's note of Churchill's remarks continued:

Hitler had admittedly declared that he had no intention of waging a
war of aggression; he, Churchill, however, was convinced that Hitler
or his followers would seize the first available opportunity to resort to
armed force.[1]

It was only against the democracies, Churchill believed, that
an aggressive Germany would turn. Hence his fear of the first
plans for an Austro-German customs union, as early as March
1931. Such an economic union, he warned, could lead only to
political *Anschluss*, and then both France and Czechoslovakia
would be in danger. As he explained, in an article syndicated
throughout the United States:

Monsieur Masaryk and Monsieur Beneš have refounded an ancient
nation. After centuries of 'bondage' they are what they call free. They
have established a strong state on the broad basis of social democracy
and anticommunism. They have three million five hundred thousand
Austrian-Germans in their midst. These unwilling subjects are a care.
But the *Anschluss* means that Czechoslovakia will not only have the
indigestible morsel in its interior, but will be surrounded on three sides
by other Germans. They will become almost a Bohemian island in a
boisterous fierce-lapping ocean of Teutonic manhood and efficiency.

Churchill could see only a single advantage in the Austro-
German plan, and that only if it were strictly limited to
economic union, without any political links. By such a move, he
wrote, the new extremism in Germany might conceivably be
controlled. In his article he explained that a success for Brüning's
foreign policy could have one important sequel, if it served to rob
'the much more dangerous Hitler movement of its mainspring',
and he went on to ask: 'Will not the mastery of Hitlerism by the
constitutional forces in Germany be a real factor in the
immediate peace of Europe? This also should be weighted.'[2]

[1] Report of a conversation, 18 October 1930, printed in full in *Churchill*, document
volume 5, 'The Wilderness Years'.
[2] Article, 'The United States of Europe', 29 March 1931, quoted in Gilbert, *Churchill*,
volume 5, page 409.

Passing through Germany in November 1932—on his way to the battlefield of Blenheim—Churchill saw the fervour of the Nazi youth. He would also have met Hitler, but for his questions to the man who was arranging the meeting: 'Why is your chief so violent against the Jews?' 'What is the sense of being against a man simply because of his birth?' 'How can any man help how he is born?'[1] Returning to Britain, Churchill told the House of Commons of the potential German threat to France, Belgium, Poland, Rumania, Czechoslovakia, and Yugoslavia:

Do not delude yourselves. Do not let His Majesty's Government believe—I am sure they do not believe—that all that Germany is asking for is equal status. I believe the refined term now is equal qualitative status by indefinitely deferred stages. That is not what Germany is seeking. All these bands of sturdy Teutonic youths, marching through the streets and roads of Germany, with the light of desire in their eyes to suffer for their Fatherland, are not looking for status. They are looking for weapons, and, when they have the weapons, believe me they will then ask for the return of lost territories and lost colonies, and when that demand is made it cannot fail to shake and possibly shatter to their foundations every one of the countries I have mentioned, and some other countries I have not mentioned.[2]

In January 1933 Hitler came to power in Germany. For six years Churchill was to warn both of the internal evils of Nazism, and of the need for the democratic States of Europe to work together in preventing the spread of Nazi power. Within three months of Hitler's triumph, Churchill warned the House of Commons against the continuing policy of disarmament, and against the British Government's pressure on France to persuade France to disarm. As Churchill declared:

When we read about Germany, when we watch with surprise and distress the tumultuous insurgence of ferocity and war spirit, the pitiless ill-treatment of minorities, the denial of the normal protections of civilized society to large numbers of individuals solely on the ground of race—when we see that occurring in one of the most gifted, learned, scientific and formidable nations in the world, one cannot help feeling

[1] Winston S. Churchill, *The Second World War*, volume 1, page 65.
[2] House of Commons, 17 November 1932.

glad, that the fierce passions that are raging in Germany have not found, as yet, any other outlet but upon Germans.[1]

For the next six years Churchill was indefatigable in his defence of democracy, and in urging the need for democracy to defend itself. All the democratic States he urged, again and again, should join together under the League of Nations, for territorial protection, and for the maintenance of internal freedom. Nor did Churchill accept the suggestions that Nazism itself might moderate, that its excesses represented the passing extravagance of all revolutions, or that British and German interests still coincided. As he wrote in a magazine article in June 1934:

This mighty people, the most powerful and most dangerous in the Western world, have reverted to the conditions of the middle ages with all the modern facilities and aggravations. We are confronted with the monstrosity of the totalitarian state. All are to think alike. No one is to disagree. To point out an obvious mistake or miscalculation is to be convicted of heresy and treason. Every link with the past, even with the most glorious traditions has been shivered. A despotism has been erected only less frightful than the Russian nightmare. Its aims are different, its forms are opposite, but its methods are the same.

Kingship and the glorious memories of bygone days are brushed aside in the interests of the newcomers who usurp all the loyalties due to the slowly woven fabric of the race. Religion must be read from the drill book. Jews must be baited for being born Jews. Little Jewish children must be insulted by regulation and routine on particular days of the week or of the month, and made to feel the ignominy of the state of life to which the Creator has called them. Venerable pastors, upright magistrates, world famous scientists and philosophers, capable statesmen, independent minded manly citizens, frail poor old women of unfashionable opinions, are invaded, bullied and brutalised by gangs of armed hooligans to resist whom is a capital offence. To be thought disloyal or even unenthusiastic to the regime which only yesterday was unknown, warrants indefinite bondage in an intern-ment camp under persecutions which though they may crush the victim, abase also the dignity of man. What a fate for Europe's strongest, most industrious and most learned sons!

Is there anything in all this which should lead us, the English

[1] House of Commons, 23 March 1933.

speaking world, to repudiate the famous chain of events which has made us what we are?—to cast away our Parliament, our habeas corpus, our rights and many freedoms, our tolerances, our decencies? On the contrary, ought we not betimes to buttress and fortify our ancient constitution, and to make sure that it is not ignorantly or lightly deranged? What a lamentable result it would be if the British and American democracies when enfranchised squandered in a few short years or even between some night and morning all the long-stored hard-won treasures of our island civilisation. It must not be.[1]

For two years, Churchill's advice was neglected: above all, his pleas for a more rapid rearmament, and his advocacy of an alliance of the democratic—and as he saw it—threatened States. As he told the House of Commons two years and three months after Hitler had come to power:

. . . if only Great Britain, France and Italy had pledged themselves two or three years ago to work in association for maintaining peace and collective security, how different might have been our position. Indeed, it is possible that the dangers into which we are steadily advancing would never have arisen. But the world and the Parliaments and public opinion would have none of that in those days.

When the situation was manageable it was neglected, and now that it is thoroughly out of hand we apply too late the remedies which then might have effected a cure.

There is nothing new in the story. It is as old as the sibylline books. It falls into that long, dismal catalogue of the fruitlessness of experience and the confirmed unteachability of mankind. Want of foresight, unwillingness to act when action would be simple and effective, lack of clear thinking, confusion of counsel until the emergency comes, until self-preservation strikes its jarring gong—these are the features which constitute the endless repetition of history.[2]

Several of Churchill's closest friends believed that Hitler's Germany did not constitute so serious a threat to Britain, or to democracy, as Churchill alleged. To one of these friends Churchill wrote, after one of Hitler's proposals for embarking on an Anglo-German understanding. 'If this proposal means that

[1] June 1934, 'Are Parliaments Obsolete?', published in *Pearson's Magazine*.
[2] House of Commons, 2 May 1935.

we should come to an understanding with Germany to dominate Europe I think this would be contrary to the whole of our history', and he added:

> You know the old fable of the jackal who went hunting with the tiger and what happened after the hunt was over. Thus Elizabeth resisted Philip II of Spain. Thus William III and Marlborough resisted Louis XIV. Thus Pitt resisted Napoleon, and thus we all resisted William II of Germany. Only by taking this path and effort have we preserved ourselves and our liberties, and reached our present position. I see no reason myself to change from this traditional view.[1]

To another close friend, Churchill wrote a year later:

> You are also mistaken in supposing that I have an anti-German obsession. British policy for four hundred years has been to oppose the strongest power in Europe by weaving together a combination of other countries strong enough to face the bully. Sometimes it is Spain, sometimes the French monarchy, sometimes the French Empire, sometimes Germany. I have no doubt who it is now. But if France set up to claim the over-lordship of Europe, I should equally endeavour to oppose them. It is thus through the centuries we have kept our liberties and maintained our life and power.
>
> I hope you will not become too prominently identified with the pro-German view. If I read the future aright Hitler's government will confront Europe with a series of outrageous events and ever-growing military might. It is events which will show our dangers, though for some the lesson will come too late.[2]

Churchill's dislike of Nazism was confirmed with every development in Germany, where persecution was a daily occurrence, and liberty of the subject suspended. In November 1935 Churchill set out the reasons for his view in an article which gave great offence to Hitler, but which told the truth as Churchill saw it. 'Two years ago', Churchill wrote:

> The Jews, supposed to have contributed, by a disloyal and pacifist influence, to the collapse of Germany at the end of the Great War, were also deemed to be the main prop of communism and the authors

[1] Letter of 12 May 1935, to Lord Rothermere, quoted in Gilbert, *Churchill*, volume 5, pages 648-9.

[2] Letter of 6 May 1936, to Lord Londonderry, printed in full in *Churchill*, document volume 5, 'The Coming of War'.

of defeatist doctrines in every form. Therefore, the Jews of Germany, a community numbered by many hundreds of thousands, were to be stripped of all power, driven from every position in public and social life, expelled from the professions, silenced in the Press, and declared a foul and odious race.

The twentieth century has witnessed with surprise, not merely the promulgation of these ferocious doctrines, but their enforcement with brutal vigour by the Government and by the populace. No past services, no proved patriotism, even wounds sustained in war, could procure immunity for persons whose only crime was that their parents had brought them into the world. Every kind of persecution, grave or petty, upon the world-famous scientists, writers, and composers at the top down to the wretched little Jewish children in the national schools, was practised, was glorified, and is still being practised and glorified.

A similar proscription fell upon socialists and communists of every hue. The Trade Unionists and liberal intelligentsia are equally smitten. The slightest criticism is an offence against the State. The courts of justice, though allowed to function in ordinary cases, are superseded for every form of political offence by so-called people's courts composed of ardent Nazis.

Side by side with the training grounds of the new armies and the great aerodromes, the concentration camps pock-mark the German soil. In these thousands of Germans are coerced and cowed into submission to the irresistible power of the Totalitarian State.

Churchill went on to ask whether Hitler shared the passions he had evoked. 'Does he', he asked, 'in the full sunlight of worldly triumph, at the head of the great nation he has raised from the dust, still feel racked by the hatreds and antagonisms of his desperate struggle; or will they be discarded like the armour and the cruel weapons of strife under the mellowing influences of success?' Churchill could give no definite answer. Those who had met Hitler, he wrote, had found him 'a highly competent, cool, well-informed functionary with an agreeable manner . . .'. The world still hoped that 'the worst' might be over, 'and that we may yet live to see Hitler a gentler figure in a happier age'. And yet, he warned, while Hitler now spoke 'words of reassurance', in Germany itself 'the great wheels revolve; the rifles, the cannon, the tanks, the shot and shell, the air-bombs, the poison-gas cylinders, the aeroplanes, the submarines, and now the beginnings of a fleet flow in ever-broadening streams from the already largely war-mobilized arsenals and factories of Germany'.[1]

Pressure for an accommodation with Nazism continued. Churchill was criticized by some of his closest friends for having written in such a way. He was portrayed by Goebbels as a man bent on war, and—by both *The Times* and Sir Samuel Hoare— as exaggerating the dangers. Even the Labour Party continued to be reluctant to follow Churchill's line of reasoning. In July 1936 he warned of those groups which Nazism 'would chastise and discipline', and he went on to explain:

I can well imagine some circles of smart society, some groups of wealthy financiers, and the elements in this country which are attracted by the idea of a Government strong enough to keep the working classes in order; people who hate democracy and freedom, I can well imagine such people accommodating themselves fairly easily to Nazi domination. But the Trade Unionists of Britain, the intellectuals of Socialism and Radicalism, they could not more bear it than the ordinary British Tory. It would be intolerable. . . .[2]

Speaking in Paris in September 1936, Churchill stressed the need to maintain parliamentary democracy, liberal civilization, and the closest possible Anglo-French co-operation. He also explained why the democracies could never submit to Nazi or Communist rule, asking his audience:

How could we bear, nursed as we have been in a free atmosphere, to be gagged and muzzled; to have spies, eavesdroppers and delators at every corner; to have even private conversation caught up and used against us by the Secret Police and all their agents and creatures; to be arrested and interned without trial; or to be tried by political or Party courts for crimes hitherto unknown to civil law.

How could we bear to be treated like schoolboys when we are grown-up men; to be turned out on parade by tens of thousands to march and cheer for this slogan or for that; to see philosophers, teachers and authors bullied and toiled to death in concentration

---

[1] Article, 'The Truth About Hitler', in the *Strand* magazine, November 1935.
[2] Speech at Horsham, 23 July 1936, quoted in Gilbert, *Churchill*, volume 5, pages 768–9.

camps; to be forced every hour to conceal the natural workings of the human intellect and the pulsations of the human heart? Why, I say that rather than submit to such oppression, there is no length we would not go to.

There were still some people, Churchill continued, who believed that the only choice for Europe was between 'two violent extremes'. This was not his view. 'Between the doctrines of Comrade Trotsky and those of Dr Goebbels there ought to be room for you and me, and a few others, to cultivate opinions of our own.' No aggression, he warned, from wherever it came, could be condoned. All aggressive action must be judged, not from the standpoint of Right and Left, but of 'right or wrong'.[1]

Politically, Churchill was very much alone at this time; but slowly, in the Trade Unions, in business circles, among the economists of the LSE, even in the Labour Party, his support for a Middle Way between Fascism and Communism was gaining ground. It was for this standpoint that Churchill looked on the Spanish Civil War. 'I refuse to become the partisan of either side', he declared. As to Communism and Nazism, he added: 'I hope not to be called upon to survive in the world under a Government of either of these dispensations. I cannot feel any enthusiasm for these rival creeds. I feel unbounded sorrow and sympathy for the victims.'[2]

In opposing Neville Chamberlain's search for a compromise with Hitler, Churchill warned the House of Commons—after the return of Lord Halifax from a visit to Hitler in December 1937:

If it were thought that we were making terms for ourselves at the expense either of small nations or of large conceptions which are dear, not only to many nations, but to millions of people in every nation, a knell of despair would resound through many parts of Europe.[3]

From the moment of Hitler's annexation of Austria, Churchill warned against allowing Czechoslovakia to be the next victim. 'To English ears', he told the House of Commons, 'the name of Czechoslovakia sounds outlandish', and he continued:

[1] Speech of 24 September 1936, printed in Gilbert, *Churchill*, volume 5, pages 787-8.
[2] House of Commons, 14 April 1937.
[3] House of Commons, 21 December 1937.

No doubt they are only a small democratic State, no doubt they have an army only two or three times as large as ours, no doubt they have a munitions supply only three times as great as that of Italy, but still they are a virile people; they have their treaty rights, they have a line of fortresses, and they have a strongly manifested will to live freely.[1]

The British Government's policy, however, was to put pressure on the Czechs to make a series of concessions to Nazi Germany, and only four days after Churchill's speech, Sir Thomas Inskip told his Cabinet colleagues, in the secrecy of the Cabinet room, that Czechoslovakia was 'an unstable unit in Central Europe', and that 'he could see no reason why we should take steps to maintain such a unit in being'. Inskip's colleagues agreed. 'Czechoslovakia was a modern and very artificial creation', said Sir John Simon, 'with no real roots in the past.'[2]

No mention was made of democracy. The remarks of the Cabinet Ministers contrasted strikingly with Churchill's assertion in 1931 of the refounding of an ancient, and now democratic state. Four months later, in September 1938, the British Government supported Hitler's demand that Czechoslovakia should actually *transfer* territory to Germany. As Churchill told the House of Commons:

The partition of Czechoslovakia under pressure from England and France amounts to the complete surrender of the Western Democracies to the Nazi threat of force. Such a collapse will bring peace or security neither to England nor to France. . . .

It is not Czechoslovakia alone which is menaced, but also the freedom and the democracy of all nations. The belief that security can be obtained by throwing a small State to the wolves is a fatal delusion.[3]

Between Munich and the outbreak of war, Churchill watched the transformation of British opinion, and its increasing influence on the Government's action. He himself spent much of his time at Chartwell, finishing a new book, a history of the English-

---

[1] House of Commons, 14 March 1938.

[2] Cabinet Foreign Policy Committee, 18 March 1938, printed in Gilbert, *Churchill*, volume 5, pages 921-2.

[3] Press Statement, 21 September 1938, printed in Gilbert, *Churchill*, volume 5, pages 978-9.

Speaking Peoples. As he wrote to one of his literary assistants in the spring of 1939:

In the main, the theme is emerging of the growth of freedom and law, of the rights of the individual, of the subordination of the State to the fundamental and moral conceptions of an ever-comprehending community. Of these ideas the English-speaking peoples were the authors, then the trustees, and must now become the armed champions. Thus I condemn tyranny in whatever guise and from whatever quarter it presents itself. All this of course has a current application.[1]

Four months later, Churchill set out his thoughts on dictatorship and democracy in a broadcast to the United States:

One thing has struck me as very strange, and that is the resurgence of the one-man power after all these centuries of experience and progress. It is curious how the English-speaking peoples have always had this horror of one-man power. They are quite ready to follow a leader for a time, as long as he is serviceable to them; but the idea of handing themselves over, lock, stock and barrel, body and soul, to one man, and worshiping him as if he were an idol—that has always been odious to the whole theme and nature of our civilization. The architects of the American Constitution were as careful as those who shaped the British Constitution to guard against the whole life and fortunes, and all the laws and freedom of the nation, being placed in the hands of a tyrant. Checks and counter-checks in the body politic, large devolutions of State government, instruments and processes of free debate, frequent recurrence to first principles, the right of opposition to the most powerful governments, and above all ceaseless vigilance, have preserved, and will preserve, the broad characteristics of British and American institutions. But in Germany, on a mountain peak, there sits one man who in a single day can release the world from the fear which now oppresses it; or in a single day can plunge all that we have and are into a volcano of smoke and flame.

'If Herr Hitler does not make war,' Churchill added, 'there will be no war.'[2]

[1] Letter to Maurice Ashley, 12 April 1939, printed in Gilbert, *Churchill*, volume 5, page 1063.

[2] Broadcast of 8 August 1939, quoted in Winston S. Churchill, *Blood, Sweat and Tears*, New York 1941, pages 163-6.

Four weeks later, Hitler invaded Poland, and both Britain and France declared war. 'This is no war', Churchill declared, 'of domination or imperial aggrandizement or material gain; no war to shut any country out of its sunlight and means of progress. It is a war, viewed in its inherent quality, to establish, on impregnable rocks, the rights of the individual, and it is a war to establish and revive the stature of man . . .'[1]

*   *   *

An essential part of Churchill's political philosophy was his belief that nothing, even in the bitterest of political controversies, must be allowed to damage the fabric of the society as a whole. It was his strong conviction that within the democratic system political disagreements, whether inside or across party, must not entail personal animosities. Such animosities would, he believed, themselves endanger the democratic process. Hence his founding of the Other Club, at the height of the political controversies of 1910. It was an attempt to bring together Liberal and Tory leaders, and other non-political figures of stature, in a fortnightly social gathering which would bridge, and indeed ignore, the political gulfs and quarrels of the day. 'Great tact will be necessary', Churchill wrote to Bonar Law, 'in the avoidance of bad moments.'[2]

The Club survived. So too did Churchill's continual efforts to maintain civility, and friendship, with political critics and opponents. 'I am confident', he had once written to one fellow Cabinet Minister, 'that our friendship will never be even ruffled by the incidental divergence of honest opinion inseparable from the perplexities of politics and affairs.'[3] This attitude included the Labour Party leaders against whom he argued so fiercely in the 1920s. When the first Labour Government came to office January 1924, Churchill at once sent Ramsay MacDonald a letter of friendship and encouragement. MacDonald replied:

[1] House of Commons, 3 September 1939.

[2] Letter of 17 November 1911. Bonar Law had just been elected leader of the Conservative Party. Quoted in *Churchill*, document volume 2, page 1337.

[3] Letter of 7 September 1908, to R. B. Haldane, quoted in *Churchill*, document volume 2, page 816.

No letter received by me at this time has given me more pleasure than yours. I wish we did not disagree so much!—but there it is. In any event I hope your feelings are like mine. I have always held you personally in much esteem, & I hope, whatever fortune may have in store for us, that personal relationship will never be broken. Perhaps I may come across you occasionally.[1]

In Parliament, Churchill, one of Labour's fiercest critics, was likewise a leading advocate of good personal relations. Throughout the Coal negotiations of 1926 he showed sympathy to the miners' grievances, and tried hard to persuade his Cabinet colleagues to force the mine-owners to accept a national minimum wage, as the miners wished. Even during the acrimonious debates which followed, Churchill's attitude, however tough, was never abrasive. 'His own laugh', wrote one Labour MP, David Grenfell, 'and the gusto with which he provokes laughter in others, are among his chief assets. He encourages the Labour back-benchers to laugh with him, rather than howl at him.'[2]

Nor was this merely a public pose. In private, Labour men knew that they could turn to him if they were in difficulties. After the death of Philip Snowden, his widow, a former suffragette and dedicated socialist, wrote to Churchill:

Your generosity to a political opponent marks you for ever in my eyes the 'great gentleman' I have always thought you. Had I been in trouble which I could not control myself, there is none to whom I should have felt I could come with more confidence that I should be gently treated.[3]

In May 1940, when Tory-Labour relations were at their most bitter, it was Churchill under whom the Labour Party was willing to serve. And it was Churchill who then brought the leading figures of the Labour movement into central positions of war policy and war direction.

*   *   *

From his first to his last political utterance, Churchill spoke of

---

[1] Letter of 27 January 1924, *Churchill*, document volume 5, 'The Exchequer Years'.
[2] *Daily Chronicle*, 19 May 1927.
[3] Gilbert, *Churchill*, volume 5, pages 857–8.

his pride in Britain and the British race. But this was not, at base, a pride in wealth or conquest—but in beneficial achievement. As Churchill saw it, Britain's most significant achievement was, as he expressed it in 1927, the 'spread of the ideas of self-government, of personal liberty and of Parliamentary institutions throughout the world'.[1] This belief in Parliamentary democracy was also a belief in the value of opinions outside the Party mould, and of Members of Parliament willing to express the unpopular view. Twenty-five years earlier, at the height of the Free Trade controversy, he had written to his constituency chairman at Oldham:

I understand the politician who, thinking only of blue or red, says 'My party, right or wrong'. But I do not understand, and therefore cannot respect, the Free Trader who sees this great danger coming upon the country and yet hesitates to use the powers with which the Constitution has endowed him to ward it off.

The government of nations is not a game of football, and when vast interests, involving the material comfort of millions of working people, and great truths quarried from the bed-rock by the toil and sacrifices of generations are assailed, those representative and responsible persons who sit by their firesides doing nothing are failing in their duty to the public.

'The decision of all this', Churchill added, 'must rest with the masses of the people. I know they wish to hear both sides of the case fully and fairly stated before making up their minds. It remains to be seen whether they will permit themselves to be manipulated by a party machine and marched this way and that way like a squad of recruits on a drill ground.'[2]

This was always Churchill's theme. Twelve years later, speaking from the opposition benches during the First World War, he implored the Government to listen to criticism. 'Ministers are often offended', he said, 'with discussions which take place in this House. The slightest opposition renders them indignant, and they are always ready to attribute mean motives to those concerned in it.'[3]

[1] Speech of 27 May 1927.
[2] *Oldham Standard*, 8 January 1904.
[3] House of Commons, 22 August 1916.

Seven months later, in advocating a Secret Session of the House of Commons, at which Ministers would explain their wartime policies in detail, Churchill declared: 'The House of Commons would be to blame and failing in its duty if upon all these great questions connected with manpower, the supply of men, and our military policy, they do not insist upon some serious discussion in which the Ministers could take part, and in which hon. Members could really address themselves to questions on which the life and fortunes of the country depend.'

Later in this same speech Churchill told MPs:

I say quite frankly, I have a feeling of despair, because it does seem to me that the House of Commons, by not grappling with these questions, by not following them up with intense attention and even ferocity, is allowing power to slip from its hands and is allowing itself to be made a useless addition to the Constitution.[1]

Churchill's strongest critics understood his genuine belief in the Constitution, and in the national wellbeing. As Josiah Wedgwood wrote to a friend in 1927: 'Baldwin seems to be getting very much under the influence of Churchill. Perhaps because C never despairs of the republic.'[2]

In June 1929 the Conservatives were defeated at the General Election, and Churchill was out of office. For ten years he was to remain in the political wilderness. But however isolated, and however abused, his faith in Parliamentary democracy never wavered. As he told an audience at Oxford University in June 1930, during the second Labour Government:

I see the Houses of Parliament—and particularly the House of Commons—alone among the senates and chambers of the world a living and ruling entity; the swift vehicle of public opinion; the arena—perhaps fortunately the padded arena—of the inevitable class and social conflict; the College from which the Ministers of State are chosen, and hitherto the solid and unfailing foundation of the executive power.

I regard these parliamentary institutions as precious to us almost beyond compare. They seem to give by far the closest association yet

---

[1] House of Commons, 5 March 1917.
[2] Letter of 4 October 1927, quoted in Gilbert, *Churchill*, volume 5, page 246.

achieved between the life of the people and the action of the state. They possess apparently an unlimited capacity of adaptiveness, and they stand an effective buffer against every form of revolutionary and reactionary violence.

It should be the duty of faithful subjects to preserve these institutions in their healthy vigour, to guard them against the encroachment of external forces, and to revivify them from one generation to another from the springs of national talent, interest, and esteem.[1]

Four years later, as the era of the National Government reduced Parliamentary opposition to a fragment, Churchill argued—as a part of that fragment—that in the modern age of great combinations, both of Labour and Capital, 'the individual must be all the more in our care', in the political as well as the social sphere. It was quite wrong, he insisted, to regard the few independent members of Parliament of that time as a 'public nuisance', or to resent 'their awkward way of thinking things out for themselves'.[2]

Churchill's concept of the middle course, the moderate centre, the role of the independent, and the supremacy of free expression was an integral part of his hatred of tyranny whether of the extreme right or the extreme left. In defending the League of Nations, and warning of Britain's own weakness *vis-à-vis* Germany, Churchill told a Conservative and business audience in 1935:

No doubt it is not popular to say these things, but I am accustomed to abuse and I expect to have a great deal more of it before I have finished. Somebody has to state the truth. There ought to be a few members of the House of Commons who are in a sufficiently independent position to confront both Ministers and electors with unpalatable truths. We do not wish our ancient freedom and the decent tolerant civilisation we have preserved in this island to hang upon a rotten thread.[3]

Churchill's advocacy of informed criticism was met by increasing reluctance on the part of the Government to divulge

---

[1] Winston S. Churchill, *Parliamentary Government and the Economic Problem*, Oxford 1930; being Churchill's Romanes Lecture, delivered on 19 June 1930.

[2] *Answers*, 31 March 1934.

[3] Speech of 26 September 1935, Gilbert, *Churchill*, volume 5, pages 668-9.

its policies, or to expose them to criticism. When, in the early summer of 1939, a debate on the Government's Palestine policy began to go badly for the Government, a three-line whip was suddenly imposed in mid-debate. Churchill was outraged. In a note which he wrote in the course of the debate, he declared:

> But what is supreme argument upon which Govt rely?
> Up till yesterday supporters of Govt
>   were summoned to Division
>   by a 2-line whip,
>   but after speech of S of S.
>   and its reception,
>   a 3rd line was added to whip.
> Not only the *Landwehr* but the *Landsturm*
>   were called out.
> That was not because case was found to be
>   unexpectedly strong.
> It was because the case was weak, and
>   because it is thought necessary to over ride argument
>   by a parade of numbers.[1]

The concept of the abdication by Parliament of its responsibilities was anathema to Churchill. When, on 2 August 1939, Chamberlain moved for a two-month adjournment, Churchill told the House of Commons: 'This is an odd moment for the House to declare it will go on a two months' holiday. It is only an accident that our summer holidays coincide with the danger months in Europe, when the harvests have been gathered, and when the powers of evil are at their strongest. . . . At this moment in its long history, it would be disastrous, it would be pathetic, it would be shameful for the House of Commons to write itself off as an effective and potent factor in the situation, or reduce whatever strength it can add to the firm front which the nation will make against aggression.'[2]

Churchill believed not only in the right of dissent to be heard, and of advice to be given, wherever it might be of service, but in the need for those who managed Parliament to maintain from day to day the highest standards of democratic procedure.

[1] Notes for a speech, 22 May 1939, printed in Gilbert, *Churchill*, volume 5, page 1071.
[2] House of Commons, 2 August 1939.

Hence his intense anger in 1934, when he learned by chance that evidence submitted to a Joint Select Committee had been withdrawn, at the request of the Committee chairman—himself a Minister—and replaced by a new and diametrically opposed version acceptable to the Government.

Yet the whole purpose of the Committee had been to examine evidence both for and against the Government's view. To tamper with such evidence was, Churchill argued, the beginning of the destruction of Parliamentary democracy. The issue itself was India, but far more, he believed, was at stake. 'These are not easy days, I think,' Churchill told the House of Commons, 'when Parliament can afford to be too lax and easygoing on the assertion of its rights and responsibilities.'[1] Of the pressures applied by the Government in causing the evidence to be changed, methods which a Committee of Privileges decided were not 'wrongful pressure', merely 'advice or persuasion', Churchill asked: 'Are these methods, quite blameless in personal honour, these methods of management and organising, to be approved indiscriminately and even applauded? Are they to be our guide in the future? Are they to be applied in every direction?'[2]

Not only tampering with evidence, but going back on solemn pledges, roused Churchill's fear for the future of Parliamentary democracy. Not for him Neville Chamberlain's suggestion for abandoning the Government's pledge on air parity with Germany—'No pledge can last for ever.'[3] As Churchill saw it, here was the British Government seeking to evade fundamental commitments because of difficulties in their path; difficulties which Churchill believed should be faced by maintaining both the pledges, and the fundamental beliefs, intact. If not, he feared that severe injury would be done to the cause which in the end would still have to be upheld. As he explained to the House of Commons during the debate on the Palestine White Paper of

---

[1] House of Commons, 16 April 1934.

[2] House of Commons, 13 June 1934.

[3] For Chamberlain's conflicts with Churchill, first when Churchill was Chancellor of the Exchequer (1924-9) and then during Chamberlain's own Chancellorship (1931-7), see Gilbert, *Churchill*, volume 5. Chamberlain's 'no pledge can last for ever' remark was made in Cabinet on 22 December 1937 (see Gilbert, *Churchill*, volume 5, page 892).

1939, when, after twenty-two years, the basic principles behind the Balfour Declaration were being abandoned:

Shall we not undo by this very act of abjection some of the good which we have gained by our guarantees to Poland and to Rumania, by our admirable Turkish Alliance and by what we hope and expect will be our Russian Alliance.

You must consider these matters. May not this be a contributory factor—and every factor is a contributory factor now—by which our potential enemies may be emboldened to take some irrevocable action and then find out, only after it is all too late, that it is not this Government, with their tired Ministers and flagging purpose, that they have to face, but the might of Britain and all that Britain means?

A few moments later Churchill returned to this theme, telling the House:

Some of us hold that our safety at this juncture resides in being bold and strong. We urge that the reputation for fidelity of execution, strict execution, of public contracts, is a shield and buckler which the British Empire, however it may arm, cannot dispense with and cannot desire to dispense with.

Never was the need for fidelity and firmness more urgent than now. You are not going to found and forge the fabric of a grand alliance to resist aggression, except by showing continued examples of your firmness in carrying out, even under difficulties, and in the teeth of difficulties, the obligations into which you have entered.

I warn the Conservative party—and some of my warnings have not, alas, been ill-founded—that by committing themselves to this lamentable act of default, they will cast our country, and all that it stands for, one more step downward in its fortunes, which step will later on have to be retrieved, as it will be retrieved, by additional hard exertions. That is why I say that upon the large aspect of this matter the policy which you think is a relief and an easement you will find afterwards you will have to retrieve, in suffering and greater exertions than those we are making.[1]

As we have seen again and again, Churchill believed that if the Government gave an honest lead, the public would follow. But it was essential, as he saw it, to face difficulties straight on; and it was because of this belief that he was able, throughout the

[1] House of Commons, 22 May 1939.

thirties, his so-called 'wilderness years', to read the warning signs as they occurred, and without any self-delusion as to what they meant.

Nor was his assertion in 1939, that handing over power to a single man was 'odious' to Anglo-Saxon civilization, a mere oratorical flourish. Although it was heartbreaking for him personally to relinquish power in 1945—believing that he had so much still to give to the peacemaking process, by means of his enormous personal authority, knowledge of past errors, good-will of so many of the world statesmen, and understanding of current and emerging problems—it was nevertheless the British people's good fortune that he was such a profound democrat, relinquishing power within hours of electoral defeat. Indeed, as he later recalled: 'The verdict of the electors had been so overwhelmingly expressed that I did not wish to remain even for an hour responsible for their affairs.'[1] That same evening he had issued a statement to the Press which included the sentence: 'Immense responsibilities abroad and at home fall upon the new Government, and we must all hope that they will be successful in bearing them.'[2]

*   *   *

'Civilization', Churchill wrote at the turn of the century, was 'a state of society where moral forces begin to escape from the tyranny of physical forces'.[3] But since the end of the First World War he had seen those moral forces themselves being challenged, not by any physical enemy, but by immoral forces of man's own making. To Bernard Shaw he wrote, in 1928, of men and women in general: 'everything they try will fail—owing to their deplorable characteristics, and their liking for these very characteristics. The only world fit for them is a Hugger Mugger world. Ants and Bees would be worthy of better things . . .'[4]

Yet Churchill believed in the ability of man to improve his situation, and to defend what had already been achieved: of

[1] Winston S. Churchill, *The Second World War*, volume 6, page 583.
[2] *The Times*, 27 July 1945.
[3] Winston S. Churchill, *Savrola*, London and New York 1900.
[4] Letter of 2 September 1928, quoted in *Churchill*, document volume 5, 'The Exchequer Years', pages 1331-2.

man in general, not mere individual leaders. Since 1940 he himself has come to epitomize the war leader, the man of the hour, the indispensable hero. But all his life he regarded such a person as having no independent existence. 'Do you think I am what I am', his fictional hero asked at the turn of the century, 'because I have changed all those minds, or because I best express their views? Am I their master or their slave? Believe me I have no illusions.'[1]

To outsiders Churchill often seemed insensitive and harsh, cynical, and brusque. His outbursts of temper, recorded by colleagues at times of incredible stress and national danger, were interpreted by some as a sign of an underlying tyrannical nature. But to those who worked closest with him, whether as Cabinet colleagues or civil servants, the quality of his mind was clear, as indeed was his overriding gentleness of character, his humour and sense of fun, as well as his deep understanding of human nature, history, and public affairs.

One civil servant, who became Churchill's Principal Private Secretary in September 1939 and remained at his side throughout the testing time of 1940, but who never became a close personal friend wrote, in retrospect, of Churchill's motive force:

... the key word in any understanding of Winston Churchill is the simple word 'Liberty'. Throughout his life, through many changes and vicissitudes, Winston Churchill stood for liberty. He intensely disliked, and reacted violently against, all attempts to regiment and dictate opinion. In this attitude, he was consistent throughout his political life. He believed profoundly in the freedom of the spirit, and the liberty of man to work out his own salvation, and to be himself in his own way. His defence of the British Government in India is not at variance with this idea; he defended British rule in India because he thought that it brought individual freedom in its train. He demanded for himself freedom to follow his own star, and he stood out for a like liberty for all men. All organised attempts to dictate to men what or how they should think, whether by the Nazis in Germany, or by the Communists in Russia, incurred his passionate hatred and fell under his anathema. In the last resort, this was the mainspring of his action.[2]

[1] Winston S. Churchill, *Savrola*, London and New York 1900.
[2] Notes by Eric Seal, Churchill's Principal Private Secretary from September 1939 to mid 1941.

This was a private opinion, not written for publication. But in August 1944 Churchill himself sent a message to the Italian people which contained, in seven questions, a compact summary of his own philosophy. The message contained seven 'quite simple, practical tests', as Churchill called them, by which freedom could be recognized in the modern world:

Is there the right to free expression of opinion and of opposition and criticism of the Government of the day?

Have the people the right to turn out a Government of which they disapprove, and are constitutional means provided by which they can make their will apparent?

Are their courts of justice free from violence by the Executive and from threats of mob violence, and free of all association with particular political parties?

Will these courts administer open and well-established laws which are associated in the human mind with the broad principles of decency and justice?

Will there be fair play for poor as well as for rich, for private persons as well as Government officials?

Will the rights of the individual, subject to his duties to the State, be maintained and asserted and exalted?

Is the ordinary peasant or workman who is earning a living by daily toil and striving to bring up a family free from the fear that some grim police organisation under the control of a single party, like the Gestapo, started by the Nazi and Fascist parties, will tap him on the shoulder and pack him off without fair or open trial to bondage or ill-treatment?[1]

Exactly fifty years had passed since Churchill had first argued publicly in favour of 'liberty of the subject'. And ten years later, in 1954, when he reprinted his Italian message in his war memoirs, he commented: 'This does not seem to require any alteration today.'[2]

A further quarter of a century has now passed, and Churchill's sense not only of the importance, but also of the fragility, of

---

[1] Quoted in Winston S. Churchill, *The Dawn of Liberation* (war speeches), London 1944, page 170. Churchill was to use this same formulation twice more, in a speech in Brussels on 16 November 1945, and to the States-General of the Netherlands on 9 May 1946.

[2] Winston S. Churchill, *The Second World War*, volume vi, London 1954, page 112.

individual liberty remains a central theme of domestic and international life. In October 1980, when the United Nations Agency, UNESCO, approved a new 'world information order', *The Times* noted that the British officials present were 'dismayed' by the results, and the paper's diplomatic correspondent went on to explain that 'British criticism emphasized the omission of "fundamental principles" such as the right to freedom of thought, opinion and expression; the free circulation of information and ideas; freedom of movement; freedom from censorship and arbitrary government control; and access to all sources of information, unofficial as well as official.'[1]

As Churchill had seen, retrogression—the flight from justice, the lapse into anarchy, the return to totalitarianism—constituted the main problem confronting the development of the twentieth century. He had expressed that view clearly in 1928, in relation to the First World War: 'Think of all these people', he wrote, '—decent, educated, the past laid out before them—what to avoid, what to do etc.—patriotic, loyal, clean, trying their utmost—what a ghastly muddle they made of it! Unteachable from infancy to tomb—there is the first and main characteristic of mankind.'[2] And yet, as Churchill wrote at the height of the Munich crisis in 1938: 'It is a crime to despair. We must learn from misfortune the means of future strength.'[3] And in his address at The Hague ten years later, in 1948, he set out yet again, as he had decade after decade for more than fifty years, the beliefs he still held, and the vision he still cherished, for mankind's future, telling the inaugural meeting of the Congress of Europe, in reiterating Roosevelt's demand for 'freedom from fear':

Why should all these hardworking families be harassed, first in bygone times, by dynastic and religious quarrels, next by nationalistic ambitions, and finally by ideological fanaticism? Why should they now have to be regimented and hurled against each other by variously labelled forms of totalitarian tyranny, all fomented by wicked men,

[1] *The Times*, 28 October 1980, report by David Spanier headed: 'Britain Dismayed by UNESCO threat to free flow of news'.
[2] Letter of 21 May 1928, Churchill to Beaverbrook, Beaverbrook papers, quoted in Gilbert, *Churchill*, volume 5, pages 1290–1.
[3] *Daily Telegraph*, 4 October 1938.

building their own predominance upon the misery and the subjuga-
tion of their fellow human beings? Why should so many millions of
humble homes in Europe, aye, and much of its enlightenment and
culture, sit quaking in dread of the policeman's knock?

That is the question we have to answer here. After all, Europe has
only to arise and stand in her own majesty, faithfulness and virtue, to
confront all forms of tyranny, ancient or modern, Nazi or Communist,
with forces which are unconquerable, and which if asserted in good
time may never be challenged again.

Churchill's aim, he added, was the emergence of 'a happier,
sunlit age', when, as he expressed it to his listeners at The
Hague, 'all the little children who are now growing up in this
tormented world may find themselves not the victors nor the
vanquished in the fleeting triumphs of one country over another
in the bloody turmoil of destructive war, but the heirs of all the
treasures of the past and the masters of all the science, the
abundance and the glories of the future.'[1]

[1] Quoted in Winston S. Churchill, *Europe Unite* (speeches 1947 and 1948), London
1950, pages 310-17.

INDEX

Compiled by the author